The Zen
Programmer

Christian Grobmeier

The Zen Programmer

Christian Grobmeier

This book is for sale at http://www.zenprogrammer.org

This version was published on 2013-11-17

ISBN 978-1493541799

To Ben Philipp

Contents

CONTENTS

Acknowledgments

I would like to thank the following people who helped me a lot while I wrote this book:

Nicole Michejew, Kathleen Weise, Boris Koch, Stephan Uhrenbacher, Upayavira. Also thank you to all who read and responded to my first post on this topic, "The 10 rules of a Zen Programmer".

This book has been edited by Zachary Low. I can highly recommend his services as he is passionate, patient, and fun to work with. You can contact him via his LinkedIn[1] page.

---

[1]http://www.linkedin.com/pub/zachary-low/40/914/51a

Preface

I am not a monk.

I have studied Zen since 2006. Seven years—it sounds like a lot. But it isn't. I am still at the beginning. I know I should live differently. But it's hard to change the life you've had for years. It's hard to see a different perspective when you are in a bad situation.

When I started with Zen, I was in a bad state but didn't know exactly what was going on. I meditated early in the morning and suddenly I recognized a few of my problems. You don't need to be ordained as a monk or become a Zen master. If you meditate you change your perspective. Ultimately it changed my mind. It changed the way I work. I became more productive and effective. But most importantly, I became happier.

I never wanted to write a book about Zen.

I saw many other software developers suffering from similar issues as I had, such as health problems or having the feeling that you don't know what you should do with the rest of your life.

Sometimes they asked me for advice. I said: "Meditate!" or: "Read about Bodhidharma." But quite often they didn't understand. Maybe because in these days we don't have the time to think about meaning when somebody tells you to meditate. Maybe because it is not easy to take the first step into something like Zen.

Actually it wasn't easy for me. I read books, yes. But that's not all you need. I sat down, yes. But I was missing something. I missed my own way. The way I lived my life. A path. I thought about who I am. Not who I want to be. But what have I done? What did I enjoy?

And the answer is music. Of all the things I did or experienced in my life, there is only one constant. I have always loved music. While the kind of music changed throughout the years, I have never stopped listening, making, or caring about music. You can easily distract me when I am playing a computer game. But it is not so easy when I listen to a fantastic album.

There once was a Zen school which practiced meditation with the Shakuhachi, a Japanese bamboo flute. I knew this ancient instrument was part of my practice. I was so happy when I realized people are still playing the Shakuhachi and furthermore, I had the chance to study together with a well-known Japanese teacher here in Germany.

I sat down and played Shakuhachi. I still do it daily. You don't need to choose art to practice Zen. You can practice Zen at any time of your life. Computer programming can be Zen practice too. I have been trying ever since I first understood this. Every day.

Computer programming alone is dangerous as practice. It's a hard job too. You can easily lose your balance. In combination with something else it might work well.

If you don't have a clue what your meditation practice should look like, just sit down on the floor. Don't search for a solution, it will find you. Don't stop thinking, it will stop itself. Just sit down until your perspective changes. The Zen mind is free of dogma. I wrote this book with that in mind. What you'll read here is my interpretation of Zen teachings. As water flows down the river, my interpretation might change in time. My understanding of Zen has been formed by a combination of experience, books, meditation, and of course the patient advice of my Sensei. It cannot serve as a generic understanding of Zen. It is my understanding at this point and time and you might agree or disagree. Feel free to adapt it to your own understanding. There is no wrong or right.

I am writing this book, because learning something about Zen often requires that you read a lot of ancient text and conduct a lot of research. Zen is a tool to be used, as is often said, but it is not easy to start using the tool. I wrote this book to give you some inspiration on how to use Zen. And I wanted it to motivate you to read more about Zen.

I got an editor for this book to help me out on spelling and grammar issues. I hope he told me about the biggest problems in my text. I believe he did. If you find something which is confusing, badly worded, or not logical, it's my own fault and I send you my deepest apologies.

Without a doubt, I support freedom, free speech, and peace. Please do not interpret otherwise just because of wording. Instead, please let me know and I will correct misleading phrases in later versions of this book.

Introduction

How I Learned to Sit Down

Many people ask me why I started with Zen. The answer is pretty easy and short: I was not enjoying my life anymore. I had constant stomach pain, a cold which never left me, and my free time consisted of drinking beer with colleagues. It looked "right," but it wasn't. And one day I promised myself to change my life, without actually knowing what was wrong.

But let me start at the beginning.

The First Years

I started as a dental technician and was happy with it. It was a tough road to get this job. I was not very interested in school. When I was twelve, I loved rock music and wanted to become a rock star. When you play drums for half the day and think about songs the other half, you do not have much time to get into math or physics. My hair grew long and then the day came where I needed a job. Not many people wanted to employ a long-haired young guy with just music on his mind. My former boss did, and I am still very thankful to him. I would still be a dental technician if the government hadn't changed everything. Medical care in Germany has become worse over the years (compared to how it was before).

When I started working on teeth, health insurance paid for a part of the cost. Of course, almost everybody took the chance to have white and beautiful teeth. But after the change, health insurance would no longer cover a single cent for most dental problems. A lot of people started to save their money and either bought the cheapest available solution or didn't care about their dental problems at all. This healthcare reform cost me my job. I was young and unexperienced and many employers kept only their experienced staff and paid them less.

A lot of people lost their jobs. This was a pretty tough experience for Germans. We were used to joining a company and working there for the next 50 years or until we died.

So I became one of the first generations after the Second World War in Germany who realized that jobs are no longer guaranteed for fifty years. I needed to do something else but had no clue what to do. It was 1998 and I was in civil service. Everybody spoke about Window 95/98 and finally I got hold of my first PC. It was an old and slow box. I wrote some letters in Word and learned about the Internet. I programmed Basic on a Commodore C64 when I was a kid and so I had an idea how to make a website for my band. We already had flyers and demotapes, but having a website would be great, I guessed. I thought FrontPage would surely help me, and so I started learning it.

But it did not. FrontPage was horrible. Somebody told me how I could write a website on my own. Again I felt the same excitement as I did when I first coded Basic. I learned

HTML and this was the start of my career. Two months later I sold two websites. The first one was paid and was well received. The second one was still in progress when we stopped it. Actually it was too hard for me: the customer wanted streaming videos and a secure login. It was a no go with my skillset. Anyway, I sold one website and published my band's website on the web.

I knew my life had changed. I learned PHP because I wanted to save time with creating websites. I coded a small music web magazine and tried to get a job as a programmer. Everybody was looking for coders and most of the employers didn't care if you had studied at university or not. If you knew what HTML was, you were a wanted person. A great bonus for a long-haired guy who had no clue about physics.

After a while I took a great job in a great company. I was lucky because the people there didn't care much about what I did *not* know. They cared about what I *knew* and explained the rest to me. This way I learned about Java, proper code, design patterns, SQL, and so on. Tomcat 3 was soon a good friend of mine.

This is where my problems slowly started emerging. As a trainee, I was less than a junior programmer, I earned only a little money. All my earnings went into the high gas prices I had to pay to travel to my job. But I needed to eat too. Therefore I accepted projects for nights and weekends which could bring in some extra money. Soon I was getting up at 6am and going to my day job. At 6pm I was back and starting my night job until I went to bed at midnight or

even later. No weekend. No fun. And yes, nearly no music.
I somehow managed to drive the 150 km to my hometown
to play once a week with my band. Everybody knew that
could not go on for long. Except me.

I worked hard as a freelancer. I had this one customer
who brought all the jobs to me. But unfortunately this
customer simply stopped paying me. He was horrible with
finances and didn't invoice his customers as he should. I
complained of course. No luck. I needed the help of experts
to get my money back after a couple months' delay. While
dealing with this issue, I could not find new customers.
That caused me more grief because I had rent to pay and
a mouth to feed. I lost a lot of energy during this time.
My girlfriend loaned me some money so I could survive
by eating only the cheapest vegetables for quite a while.
This way I managed to finish my training and could take
my final exams for programming. I was a new and hungry
programmer.

A new surprise would not be far off. I had hoped to get
a job where I trained. But my company went bankrupt and
so I had to get a new job again.

The Job I Did Everything For

Can you imagine how it feels if you are totally out of
money, your fridge is empty, and you just lost your job?
Panic is not a good word for it. It's more tangible. I was
afraid of the future. I wanted to get out of this situation
and never return. I decided it was time to get a job which
improved my CV and agreed to a contract with a huge

consulting company.

My first project was in Frankfurt, which was six hours away by car. I rode the train up every Monday morning, worked more than sixty hours and traveled back on Friday after lunch. I slept for a long time on Saturday and behaved like a zombie, and could not relax on Sunday as I had to prepare for the next week.

The project was well known as one of the worst. Eighty people tried to stop the ship from sinking. It was a huge mess and highly complex. We had a vision of cleaning up the code. We tried. We changed a system which was huge. The chance you could break something was very high. People were nervous and some of them started to behave like idiots at work.

Every line of written code comes with a lot of emotions. Try to tell your colleague he wrote bad code when he is giving his best. A good number of developers left the company. But I couldn't. I had to stay. I believe you need to stay more than two years in a company to be taken seriously.

While our cleanup was progressing, people changed. The team became smaller and better communication was possible. After all, we had a team who liked each other. We still worked a lot, but then there were times when we stopped working late in the evening and went out for a drink or two and ate some great food. When you get drunk after a long working day you no longer feel like a slave under pressure. You feel more like a rock star who can save the world. It is just *you* who can save the company and your colleagues. When one of the company partners pays for your drinks you feel even more important.

After I lived like this for two years I suddenly became very tired. My job was no fun anymore. I didn't feel like a coding rock star anymore. My band was at its end. I had not found the power to keep it alive or to be creative. Sometimes I coded Open Source when I went to my hotel after work. After fourteen hours of work you can squeeze another couple hours out when you have had enough beer. But I had no energy for music. I hadn't had the time for rehearsing, composing new songs, or going on tour. I had lost all passion for traveling (which was never very strong to begin with). I was just glad when I could go home and sleep. My band split up after eleven years and not on good terms.

While I was waiting for the train each morning I asked myself: Is this life? It was horrible. I managed to become a respected team member. I coded for somebody I didn't know and when the project was done, I was history. I had no money problems anymore. My life consisted of work and beer. There was no art, no music. Maybe it's OK for some, but I didn't want to live like that for the rest of my life.

One day my project decided to move its location to Munich. This was closer to where I was living. I thought everything would be better. But it wasn't. I was out early in the morning and returned late at night. Zombie-Life, reloaded. I didn't see any light at the end of the tunnel. It just went on and on, day after day.

My life needed to change. I felt it, but I wasn't sure what to do nor what was wrong. I mean, many people live like that. Go to work, drink beer, repeat. I thought something was wrong with me.

One morning I remembered that I had once tried meditation when I was fourteen. A friend loaned me a book which he had borrowed from his parents. He said, it was about meditation and that maybe it would help me to be more enthusiastic about school. I tried it, and it was cool, but didn't help me with school.

One morning I woke up early. My coworkers and I had worked hard and my brain could not relax. I was dreaming of source code and, at 5 a.m., I went into my living room and opened the window. A fresh breeze welcomed me. The morning air had a fantastic taste since there were no cars around. It was silent; birds started to sing their early songs. I did not plan it. I remembered my friend's book and then I sat down on the floor and stared into the shadows. My goal was to stop thinking for a short while. I couldn't stand it. My heart was already beating fast. And I didn't want it to be like that. In my head I heard my manager's chatter. It was louder than the birds. But after a while it became quiet and the birds' songs were the only noise.

On that day, I bought two books about Zen. Many books on meditation were about "spirituality", "mysticism", or "religion". But hey, I was just a programmer! I didn't want to adopt a new religion, I wanted to learn about meditation. The chatter in my head should shut up.

Luckily I quickly learned that Zen is not so much about

mythology. It's not about worship. This is why I looked into it. I read the books and liked them. But reading the books didn't help me. Zen is about practice and only practice helped me. In this book I have discussed the practice which I started with. Meanwhile, I wanted more Zen. It changed my mind completely. But this is not what you can read here. I will tell you what I did when my head exploded. My hope is, it will help you too. Whether you continue with it or not is not relevant to this book. Other than a few words on the history of Zen you'll see that I do not require you to change your beliefs.

This was the way I found Zen. I quit the company and went to another one. After a while, I was working at an exhausting level again. It took me a couple of years to recognize this. At one point I realized that I was working against my own business ethics. Then something changed in me and my Zen practice began to bear blossoms.

At the end of 2010, I left my job. I rejected several high paid offers to found my own company. My business (Time & Bill[2]) and some freelance services I provided brought less cash in than I could have made in a company. But I worked mostly from home and saw my kid grow up. That was more than anyone could have paid me.

After a long dark period I finally got my life back under control. I still work my sixty hours, but I do not complain any longer. I am done with self-pity and am able to enjoy the good parts and the bad parts as well (or at least I try). I have learned that not everything that was bad in the past

---

[2]http://www.timeandbill.de

was tied to the job.

But I also have learned that some things in life are simply time wasters which one does not need to follow.

Now, that's my story—at least a part of it. Let's look at some history.

What Is Zen?

Who Was Siddharta Gautama?

Siddharta Gautama founded what we know as Buddhism. He was born in 563 BCE as the son of King Suddhodana. Prophecies said that he would either become a mighty king or a holy man, a world teacher.

His father preferred to see Siddharta sitting on his throne and tried to hide everything bad of this world from him. Suddhodana thought if his son believed the world was a place of only good things, Siddharta would decide to inherit the throne instead of having the idea to become a holy man. He banned everything which was withering, old, or ugly from the palace and forbid Siddharta from going outside. Locked in the palace of his father, Siddharta grew up and married Yasodhara, with whom he had a son, Rahula.

One day he managed to get out of the protected palace gardens. He traveled on a chariot accompanied by his charioteer, Channa.

On their journey Siddharta saw a crippled old man who suffered from his age and wounds. Siddharta asked Channa why the old man was suffering. Channa explained that aging is something which happens to every person. Every one of us will become weak one day and suffer from aging.

Then they saw another man, sick with fever. Channa explained that sickness is part of our life and we can't avoid suffering from it.

Finally they saw a corpse near the street. Channa said we all must die at the end. Life will end for everybody at some point, rich or poor. We all will die.

Siddharta despaired. While they were traveling back, they saw an ascetic. Channa told Siddharta that this man was trying to find a way out of misery. Hearing this, Siddharta had hope again. He believed that there must be a way to end suffering.

Siddharta now understood that aging, sickness, death, and pain were connected to life and couldn't be separated from it. This knowledge is called the four insights.

With this knowledge in mind, Siddharta Gautama left his family to find out how humans could find a way out of this cycle of despair. With this decision he became the founder of Buddhism. He had a spectacular life, living as an ascetic and nearly starving to death.

Eventually he reached enlightenment by sitting for three days and nights in meditation under the Bodhitree.[3] From then on he taught his way to students until he died from food poisioning. He became the first Buddha of his

---

[3]You can still visit the Mahabodhi Temple near Patna, India, and see the holy tree where he achieved enlightenment.

time[4] and is subject to many myths and legends.

Is Siddharta's Teaching Compatible with Other Religions?

Absence of God

Buddhism is a religion without a god. Siddharta himself was not a prophet. He was not sent from God, nor was he a mystical being like an angel. In his lifetime, he always wanted to be seen as what he was—a mortal.

The most important practice in Buddhism is meditation. And in fact, meditation is not unknown to the Catholic Church, where it is often practiced in monasteries. It is also known in Islam, or more specifically in Sufism, where it is called Dhikr.

The absence of a God, the fact that Siddharta was human (and he called himself a human), and practices which are not unknown to other religions, make it easy to connect Buddhism to other religions like Islam or Christianity. I have heard of Catholic priests who also became Zen priests.

One can doubt that these religions are compatible when they watch TV and see Buddhists in orange clothing practicing some kind of rituals and "praying". Actually there are some—or maybe many—Buddhist lineages which

---

[4]Some say Siddharta Guatama was the fourth Buddha. There were probably even more before him and there will certainly be more after him. Gautama Buddha became one of the most popular Buddhas because he was the first Buddha in written history. After his death, his students taught what they learned to others. Eventually his teachings were written down.

do so. Buddhism is not only one thing like Catholicism is. You could compare it to Christianity as a whole, which describes not only Catholics alone, but also Protestants or other Christian groups. The same goes for Islam. There is one central teaching (Qur'an) with different interpretations such as Sunni Islam and Shi'a Islam.

One Buddha, Many Buddhas

When Siddharta Gautama became enlightened, people started to call him "Buddha". Buddha is a title which means "the awakened one". His full name would actually be Siddharta Gautama Buddha, but he is often referred to as just Buddha.

In the Buddha's teachings everything is based on the concept of the "middle way", where no extreme positions find a place. Others who have followed this middle way and mastered it became enlightened too and thus received the title of Buddha. Every Buddha had his own views and at some point in time the teachings started to differ. The "core", Gautama Buddha taught, stayed the same, but the way to reach the end of suffering is different. You could also say, Buddhism is in some ways a living religion; there are also Buddhas in the modern age who translate the sayings of Buddha for us into our modern world.[5]

---

[5]Please note, even when I try to translate Buddhism to the programming world, I am far from being Buddha. I am speaking of others, great teachers like Kôdô Sawaki.

Rituals and Praying

In Tibet there are a lot of rituals, much veneration of sacred objects, and many other religious practices. Some Buddhists actually pray to Buddha as a god. I actually don't know why they do things like that. If they are actually praying to some being and expecting it to listen or even to help, they interpret Buddhism differently than I. I understand that Buddha taught that everybody must end his suffering through his own power. I might be wrong on that. But it gives you one reason why I am not following this path. Please note, that a few very popular Buddhist schools, like "Pure Land", consider the deistic element crucial.

Even when considering a more mystical aspect like rebirth, worshipping doesn't make sense to me. Maybe you have heard that some Buddhists believe they are reborn as long as they cannot end their suffering. When they finally manage to break this cycle of birth and death, they are going to Nirvana. I am not sure if a Buddha who went to Nirvana will listen to us from there. Actually I believe they are no longer in a specific form. That's just my take on it, but for me Buddha has died. We already have everything we need from him, now it is our own turn to help ourselves out of suffering.

I am very happy that worshipping and praise in Zen are minimal. While there are rituals, they have nothing to do with falling into a trance, praying and crying for salvation, or something like that. The rituals I know just make sure you don't forget your way and you don't forget the importance of your practice. Actually I am a very skeptical person and it would not be easy for me to perform some of the rituals I have seen in Tibet. My guess is most of the readers of this book will feel the same.

The "rituals" I follow include the way we practice Zazen (sitting meditation) and Suizen (meditation with flute). This includes wearing proper clothing and on special occassions using joss sticks. I treat everything I need for my practice with respect. This includes my Zazen pad. While the image of a guy treating his sitting pad with respect may make you smile, it is actually very important for me to get in the mood for meditation and concentration. All rituals seem to help you get the right concentration. When you are done with it, your mind is clear and you can start with the real, hard practice of meditation.

One of the first people to read an early version of this manuscript mentioned, "rituals simply grant meaning to otherwise trivial actions, and that can be a useful thing." We'll come back to Zen Programmer's rituals later in this book.

Religion or Philosophy?

I know a bunch of people who think Buddhism is more of a philosphy than a religion. If you like, you can think like that. Personally I have found many reasons why I call it a religion. I do not have the competence to write a long text on this debate. After all, it is up to you to find the right term for it.

Why do I think Buddhism might be a religion?

There is no god and the rituals and prayers often have

a symbolic character rather than to worship an existing entity. Actually you'll find some things in the first Buddha's teaching which you can call a mystic aspect of Buddhism. There is no proof that it's possible. You either believe it or not. These aspects make Buddhism a religion.

Two examples:

Buddha said with Buddhism you can find an end to suffering. The suffering of age, death, sickness, and pain can find an end. If you are in a horrible situation—maybe a bad car accident—and suffer from extreme and constant pain you will understand quickly why Buddhism is a religion. You really need to *believe* you can find an end to suffering if you are in such an situation.

When a Christian dies, he'll be judged by God and go to either Heaven or Hell.[6] In Buddhism there is no Hell as it is known from the Bible. The ultimate goal is to become one with the universe again and vanish completely. You need to break the circle of life and death and stop being reborn. When you are one with the universe you'll find peace.

Practicing Does Not Turn Your World Upside Down

The good thing is, you don't need to believe in reincarnation to practice Zen. You don't even need to care what happens after death. You could take many of the mystical aspects of Buddhism as symbolic and abstract and stick

---

[6]As far as I know, the Bible doesn't speak of an eternal Hell either. It seems that the Catholic Church teaches of an eternal Hell, while the Bible itself only speaks of a temporary Hell, known as the Purgatory. I apologize for not being more accurate here and leave it to the interested reader to learn more.

with the teachings of your religion.

You can study the original teachings of Gautama Buddha or other Buddhas and you will most likely not find anything which speaks against the teachings of Jesus Christ or the Prophets of Islam. Of course, I cannot know about all religions out there. There are religions like Asatro or Shinto, which are very difficult to compare. Anyway, if your current religion is a peaceful one, chances are good that nothing Gautama Buddha said conflicts with your beliefs.

For the Zen Programming book I have tried to adapt some practices which can be performed in the office. You'll not find anything in this book which aims to make you a Buddhist.

Decide for Yourself

After reading these arguments, what is the conclusion?

You need to decide it yourself.

Religion often differs from person to person. I have an agnostic, almost atheistic position. In my world, deities do not matter much. I do believe in what Buddha said but I couldn't live with "Pure Land" Buddhism.

You need to look into your own heart and decide, if your beliefs are in conflict with Buddha's teachings. Certainly it is not easy to believe in Buddhist lineages which rely on the deistic element.

The good thing is you can still learn from all Buddhas without taking on all the aspects. Treat it in the way that it fits for you.

But What Is Zen Actually?

In the previous sections I used the term Zen in conjunction with Buddhism. Actually Zen is a specific lineage of it, like Tibetan Buddhism. Like Buddhism, Zen has it's own story. Bodhidharma was an impressive monk from India. He brought Ch'an to China which became Zen. He is often referred to as the founder of Zen. In addition he is said to have founded Shaolin Kung-Fu.

Bodhidharma is the subject of many myths and legends. One of the most famous legends says he sat nine years in front of a wall to meditate. When he became tired, he was so angry with himself that he cut off his eyelids and threw them away. Where the lids hit the ground, the first tea plants grew. Today it is traditional to drink tea during meditation breaks to keep the practicing people awake. This legend does not only show what an impact Bodhidharma still has, it also shows how dedicated Bodhidharma was. This strictness is being found in all Zen groups and of course in the Shaolin groups as well.

Bodhidharma explained what Zen is pretty well:

> Not thinking about anything is Zen. Once you know this, walking, standing, sitting, or lying down, everything you do is Zen.
>
> —Bodhidharma (Red Pine, 1987)

Another Zen master explained it a bit differently:

Buddhism means: "no I" and "nothing to gain". You
need to be one with the universe and all life.

—Kôdô Sawaki (Sawaki, 2005)

Zen masters often use irrational arguments to explain
Zen. These two quotes are more of the rational kind. Bodhidharma said we need to defeat our mind, which often acts
like a monkey or a horse. The monkey's mind jumps from
one topic to another, without control. The horse's mind has
a horse's will and moves forward, no matter what. Without
monkeys and horses in our mind, we can have a Zen mind.
No need to think about nasty managers, unpaid bills, or
the idiot at the other desk, who just committed a bunch of
flawed code.

Sawaki Roshi said there is no "I" and nothing to gain.
Our thoughts are misleading. Why do we want the new
car when our old one still works? Will it really make us
any happier? Is life better when we drive a new car? Do we
want to impress somebody?

Zen is a mirror of our selves. When you practice Zen
meditation, you'll find your way back to your self. You'll
get your feet back on the ground again and won't worry
about all the nonsense any longer.

In the past, some people thought Zen monks could fly.
Actually if you watch some Japanese movies you can see

meditating people lift off from the ground. If you ask Kôdô
Sawaki what Zen could give you, he would say:

> Zen does not give you anything.
>
> —Kôdô Sawaki (Sawaki, 2005)

Other Zen masters would probably say: sure, Zen can
make you fly. And they are well aware that from a physical
standpoint you'll never fly. The problem with Zen is, if you
try to understand it in a rational way, you'll fail. Zen is not
about logic and rational processes to better your life. It's
about letting go of your wishes and desires and living your
life without senseless distraction. Zen lets you live now. No
need to wait for tomorrow.

The philosophy behind it is sometimes pretty radical.
If you do not listen carefully to your master (or have the
wrong master) you'll probably think Zen is about giving up
yourself and letting go of humanity. But it's different. Zen
is about you. It does not give you anything, as Kôdô Sawaki
said, because you already have everything. Zen helps you
to get rid of the dust of your mind which is preventing you
from looking at yourself.

It is nearly impossible to explain with words what Zen
is. You need to practice and hopefully you will understand
what wise men like Sawaki Roshi or Bodhidharma meant.
Zen is something you need to experience.

On Buddhism

This chapter will give you an introduction to Buddhism. It is brief and surely not complete. While you'll read about some myths and Buddhas doctrines, you'll also find a couple of personal experiences in here. You can say this is what I first experienced when starting to study Buddhism. It made me think.

Hell and the Four Noble Truths

In a Zen book I once read, I was pretty much surprised that the author wrote about a "Hell" (Jap: 奈落 Naraku). For me it was difficult to understand how a word, which I connected to the Christian religion in the first place, related to Zen. In other texts I found out that the Buddhists' "Hell" is different. At first I was shocked to hear Hell is not where you are sent after death for punishment—it's something you are born in. One's life a life in Hell? It sounded strange.

As already mentioned, it is easy to mix Zen with other religions or philosophies. Over the years, Japanese Zen has been enriched with myths and legends of Shinto and stories from ancient Japan. It is not easy to find out what is an actual teaching of Buddha and what is a legend or interpretation of a fable.

Later my Sensei[7] explained it to me.

Siddharta Gautama had learned aging, sickness, death, and pain were ultimately connected to life—the four insights. With that in mind it should be surprising people run after money and power their whole life.

> You die naked.
>
> —Kôdô Sawaki (Sawaki, 2005)

When Siddharta became Buddha, he taught us the four noble truths. Without exception, all forms of Buddhism consider this as a core belief.

1. One must understand that to live is to suffer (Dukkha Sacca). It is a diagnosis of our existence: we now know that we'll never be satisfied and therefore will suffer.
2. The root causes for our suffering are Greed, Hate, and Delusion (Samudaya Sacca). Where do they dwell? In our own mind, in what we demand.
3. Suffering will disappear when the root causes go away. One needs to overcome the causes of suffering (Nirodha Sacca). It is like fixing a filesystem bug and then having the UI work.

---

[7]A Sensei is like a teacher. You can read more about it in the section Teacher and Student.

4. The eightfold path will lead you to overcome suffering (Magga Sacca). This is a hands-on way to solve the issues of your mind.

Think of Ebenezer Scrooge, the greedy old man of Charles Dickens's "A Christmas Carol". Ebenezer was not happy man before he met the Christmas ghosts. He never laughed. Nobody liked him. And he was constantly afraid of becoming poor. What other than Hell is that life?

We could say we all live in Hell. But luckily there is a way out: the Eightfold Path. We'll come to it.

Why are the four noble truths mentioned in a book for programmers? Because we are suffering like everybody else. We have our own Hell, when we go to office. We want the next great job or are afraid to fail in a project or maybe we try to get more money out of our customers, because they urgently need us.

The Gadget Ghost

Another term which you can find often in Zen literature is "Ghost"; for example, "Hungry Ghosts". These ghosts are well known in China where the dead return to the houses of their families, hungry as the name suggests. Unlike Western Zombie movies, in China the ancestors serve their visitors food and drinks at the "Hungry Ghost Festival".

In Japan there are two different kind of ghosts, Gaki (餓鬼) and Jikininki (食人鬼). They have many of the characteristics of Persian Ghouls or what in Western movies are referred to Zombies.

> Know, reverend Sir,
>
> that I am a jikininki—an eater of human flesh.
>
> [...]
>
> And because of this selfish impiety I was reborn, immediately after my death, into the state of a jikininki.
>
> Since then I have been obliged to feed upon the corpses of the people who die in this district.
>
> —Lafcadio Hearn (Hearn, 1904)

I have been told that a hungry ghost must not necessarily be dead. This term can also be used on living people, not only on walking nightmares. Hungry Ghosts—greedy people who live in their own Hell.

If you are Ebenezer Scrooge, you are lucky. As a fictional character, your life is easy to fix. But in reality it is not so easy. Ask yourself: what makes you suffer? What ghosts are inside and outside of you, and what is the kind of Hell in which you are living? The Career Hell? The Self-Esteem Hell?

I have my own Hell of course. Sometimes I desperately want a new tablet computer. I don't need it, really. I need food, water, and a safe place to sleep. But my best friend got one recently and it looks fantastic. Suddenly I wanted one myself. Bad luck, since I was out of money at the time. Why am I such a poor guy without the money I need? Why does it look like everybody else has got a better life than me?

I called the ghost inside me the "gadget ghost". Since I identified it, I can live with it. I know a tablet would eat up my time. Since I don't have a tablet, I probably have more time to enjoy dinner.

Don't the ghosts make us humans? Sure they do! As we know humans suffer. You decide if you are OK with suffering or if you want to stop it. You don't need to get rid of all your desires to become a better programmer. But it helps you to reflect on your ghosts.

Some of us want to suffer. Suffering has become a habit for them. Sometimes they are simply afraid of change—they prefer the devil they know. Instead of starting to change their situation or accepting it, they simply stay in their mood. For humans it is necessary to suffer from time to time. We can allow ourselves to suffer here and there. But there is also a time when we need to stop our suffering and act against it. We need to prevent developing a habit out of suffering. On the other hand we can't always be happy. Happiness and suffering both come and go. We need to find a balance between suffering and happiness: the middle way. Knowing about your own ghosts, when to enjoy and when to defeat them, will help you to find your balance and your personal middle way.

Zen Monks prefer to stay poor for a good reason—they want to end their suffering and end the cycle of death and birth. You need to choose how far you want to go.

The Eightfold Path

The Buddha said we need to follow the eightfold path to end suffering. It is more or less a tutorial how to fix your life. The Eightfold Path cannot be compared to The Ten Commandments. They are not commands; they are principles you can follow. In programming terms, they are the best practices. There is no "must". You can adopt these recommendations or not. You will not be punished with going to Hell after death.

If you decide to minimize your suffering, then it is a pretty good thing to follow the Eightfold Path as much as possible. It is not a fixed path with static "do" or "don't". The Buddha said his path is the middle way, and as such the Eightfold Path can be seen.

I will give a short overview of this path, as I consider it crucial to understand. It helps us in our daily work in the office and in general. My interpretation shown here is reduced and minimal for the use of programmers mainly. I do not elaborate all aspects of the path, it is the work of the Zen priests to explain it to us. Also I don't want to start a scientific debate on "the four different forms of thinking", which would ultimately lead me to compare the Buddhist view to the knowledge I gained from university when I studied Psychology. But this is not the purpose of this book.

If you want to read more about the Eightfold Path, I refer you to "The Buddhism Primer".(Dhammasaavaka, 2005)

The Right View

The core of the right view is to understand the Four Noble Truths. Not only in theory, but from the bottom of your heart. It means, you understand the things as they are, not as they pretend to be. It does mean that you understand why you suffer and when and that you understand how you can fix your issues.

This can be interpreted very differently. Even though the "Right View" does sound pretty abstract, it is of much value.

For example:

When Paul is working on some code, Mike comes into the office and shows him a brand new smartphone. Soon a bunch of people are around Paul and Mike. The phone has a fascinating new screen and it is the latest model you can have. Nobody knows how Mike managed to get this phone, because it is not yet for sale. And it is very expensive, only a few people can afford it. As a father of two kids, Paul surely would not have the money to buy it.

Some people may think: why Mike? Why not me? Paul is one of them, but with the right view he understands to live is to suffer. It is natural. Even if Paul should get such a phone, the suffering would not end. New problems would arise. The owner of such a phone surely needs to protect it well from thieves. After all, Paul knows it doesn't matter if he has such a phone or not. He starts to overcome his suffering and congratulates Mike who in turn tells him an interesting story about how he could get one.

Another example:

Paul comes back to his desk, facing a very aggressive email from his boss, Joe. Not enough, a few minutes later Paul's boss appears at his desk, shouting at him. Paul left the office late at 2am, fixing a problem. He delivered a bugfix version to his customer after seventeen hours of work. A beer and a shower later he fell to bed, exhausted. He was back in the office at 10am, one hour later than usual, and started the day by chatting with Mike about his new telephone.

Joe becomes angry because Paul was late and seems to be lazy. He tells him that others would surely love to have his job. Paul explains he was in the office until 2am and fixed a huge problem, but Joe doesn't care. At 9am everybody needs to be in the office. He screams. After all, it is Joe's opinion that it is Paul's fault that he wrote such buggy code which he needs overtime to fix it. If Paul didn't always break dress code and get distracted by his MP3-player, these kinds of problems wouldn't happen.

Sadly this is a true story. I wasn't Paul, but sat next to him. Paul was a very nice guy and couldn't even respond to Joe, although the whole situation was absolutely unfair. Finally Paul apologized and promised to work an hour longer on that day.

The right view doesn't mean to endure the behavior of Joe. But it means to look at the situation and understand what happened. Why was Joe so unfair?

He was fighting hard to keep his company running. He always accepted low budget projects and he paid his employees the same. This resulted in an unbelievable time pressure and fluctuation of employees. He surely didn't have the time to reflect on his problem and continued with it while the situation became worse day after day. Every night when he went to sleep, Joe most likely had his head full of sorrows. And then his employee comes into office later than usual. He fixed a problem he originally caused. The customer is glad to have the fix, but what will he think? That the company only employs losers? More sorrows! Actually the programmer should not have caused that problem and the additional load of sorrows. Since Joe doesn't have the right view, he cannot help himself from acting aggressive and putting the sorrows back to the (so-called) root cause of the problem.

Maybe I am wrong with my interpretation as stories from the real life are often more complex than they seem at first glance.

With the right view, Paul would understand why his boss reacts like that. The right view tells us that there is more than just one view (like saying Joe is a born idiot). Paul unfortunately didn't have the "right view" on this situation. He was very afraid of losing his job. He also thought he did something terribly wrong and finally he thought Joe was right, even when others told him it was not the case.

Please remember, the "right view" is not the "correct view". The right view would have told Paul that there is no need to suffer. The correct view would compare facts and give a complete analysis of the situation and conclude with "wrong" and "right". But there is nothing like "wrong" or "right", so you can't say you have the "correct view" on things.

Right Intention

The right intention is the way we do things. Buddha taught us that we should perform our actions without our desires. We should have good will and resist anger. We should not act cruel, aggressive, or do harm to others.

When Paul went to Mike's desk and spoke about his new phone this action seemed to be fine. A nice chat is a nice chat. But the intention could be to do harm. Maybe Paul would try to get some information about the phone and spread nonsense about how selfish, arrogant, and rich Mike is.

Your intention is impacting you, whether you are doing nasty things or not. Aggressive feelings are a result of your own suffering. As long as you don't fix your feelings, you simply can't stop your suffering. When you are acting with wrong intention you are doing not only harm to others, you are also doing harm to yourself.

When you code with aggression you run the risk of introducing bugs. It is dirty code. Negative emotions take brain processing time from you. When a Zen programmer writes code, he only writes code. If his mind is full of aggression he cannot write only code.

When your intentions are bad you need to solve your issues before going back to work. Apply the right view, or try to speak with somebody.

Another, more subtle example.

When I was once meditating I heard something going on in the room next door. Apparently my wife had a small accident there, because after some kind of noise I heard her cursing. I could have stood up and asked if she was in need of some help. Or I could have considered meditation practice as more important and just continued. I remembered a story from Jiho Sargent (Sargent, 2001). She tried to meditate in a lone place. But the birds disturbed her concentration. She became angry and closed the window but the noise kept on. Then she realized that the birds were part of her practice.

My wife is part of my practice. When somebody needs help it is impossible to meditate because your intention is not right. Your practice becomes dirty. Zen is practice and Zen cannot be done behind monastery walls alone. Zen has it's place in the real world and that means there are birds singing and there are people who need your help.

I helped and earned a "thank you" from my wife. My practice was not interrupted too much and I could continue with a clear mind.

Remember that story, when you try to do Zen programming in your office. You need to stay connected to the real world and can't ignore others. It is usually not a good idea to drink coffee when the team is in trouble. It is also not good to think Zen programming practice is more important than helping others, when they need it.

Right Speech

The Buddha knew that the wrong words can cause war, despair, grief, or make enemies. He told us we should speak the truth and in a friendly and warm manner. Also he did tell us we should speak up only if necessary.

In the popular blog post "The Ten Rules of the Zen Programmer" I wrote:

Shut up.

This refers to the right speech. Furthermore I believe one should try not to get on somebody else's nerves. The reason is very obvious. Imagine a colleague who always comments on what you say in a team meeting.

From the Dhammapada (Buddha, 1986):

Bhikkhus![a] A bhikkhu must have control over his tongue; his conduct must be good; his mind must be calm, subdued and not flitting about as it pleases.

—Buddha

[a] The followers of Buddha were called Bhikkhu in ancient days; nowadays you could more or less translate it as "monk".

Again in the Dhammapada, the Buddha continues with

the verse:

> The bhikkhu who controls his mouth (speech), who speaks wisely with his mind composed, who explains the meaning and the text of the Dhamma—sweet are the words of that bhikkhu.
>
> —Buddha

In today's world it is very difficult to shut up. Social networks give us the chance to comment on everything all the time. Our thoughts are taken throughout the whole world in minutes. Sometimes we comment on or "+1" a photo which we haven't looked for longer than a second. We hit the like button way quicker than we think. We don't care on the implications of our action. Today we are surrounded by a lot of nonsense which we really don't need.

If we all would apply the "right speech" to how we work with social networks, we would not read so often that somebody needs to go out with the dog, has a bad hangover, or dislikes his breakfast.

Words can ruin the life of others—written or spoken. At the very least it can hurt feelings and make enemies. You need to consider wisely what you say or write. If you do that at work, you will find it a more friendly place.

The right speech means to:

• Speak the truth and do not lie.

- Abandon divisive speech: avoid rude words, use gentle speech.
- Abandon abusive speech: no slandering, promote friendliness and unity.
- Stay away from idle chatter.

Even when your project is in trouble you'll see that friendly words will help to turn unmotivated and frustrated people into diligent positive thinkers who are eager to help solve the problem(s).

The Buddha said we should tell the truth.

How far should it go? If you are familiar with Immanuel Kant's "Metaphysics of Moral" (Kant, 2004) you know why I am asking that. Kant's "Categorial Imperative" brings dilemmas like the following to the table:

A murderer knocks on your door. He suspects his victim is a guest of your house and asks for him. If you knew about his murderous intentions, what would you say? Lie and avoid the death of your guest? Or would you speak the truth?

Kant thinks we should tell the truth and tell the killer about our guest. If you lied, the term "truth" would become worthless. The question is whether you would be guilty of the murder. Who knows, says Kant. If you lie, the murderer could kill you too, if he finds out. Even worse, he could find his victim hidden in the London tube and kill him there. The panic might lead to the death of many. Kant would blame you for that if you lie. As we cannot know what the future brings, Immanuel Kant recommends us to always speak the absolute truth.

I cannot tell if Gautama Buddha described categorial imperative hundreds of years ago. We programmers hopefully do not get into such dilemmas where it comes to life or death.

Bad speech can become much worse than Kant's Dilemma:

Accipere fidem est voluntatis, sed tenere fidem iam acceptam est necessitatis.

—Thomas Aquinas

Which would mean something like:

Having faith is voluntary, but keeping to that faith is necessary.

—Thomas Aquinas

Thomas Aquinas explained that we can choose our beliefs freely. But if we have chosen, we need to stick with it. He asked for the death penalty for heretics. With his violent speech he is considered the root cause of the Inquisition, who killed thousands in ancient days.

Move away from the past and other situations look more familiar:

Consider a programming team wants to deliver to their

customer. Before they are able to do so, something goes wrong with the automated unit tests. The code looks OK, but the build system itself appears to be broken. It is not easy to find out what happened, because everybody in the team shares the same login to your system. Angela and Tom are asked to fix the issue. The issue becomes hot and, after a while, Tom tells Angela that he might have caused the issue the other day. He asks her not to tell anybody, because he is afraid to lose his job. Angela agrees and together they are able to fix the issue with Tom's information. Later their boss comes to Angela's desk and asks about the root cause of the problem—and he looks very angry.

What should Angela say?

I think there is no good answer. Angela promised Tom not to speak about his fault; on the other hand she should speak the truth. Maybe the best answer is to say that she would tell the person in charge but cannot reveal the name because of a promise. I can imagine her boss would become mad about it.

Software projects today are not only code as people would think. These days it's based a lot on communication. The "right speech" has become crucial to every participant of the project.

Right Action

The second ethical principle, right action, involves the body as natural means of expression, as it refers

> to deeds that involve bodily actions. Unwholesome actions lead to unsound states of mind, while wholesome actions lead to sound states of mind.
>
> —Dhammasaavaka (Dhammasaavaka, 2005)

If you do the wrong things, your mind will give you hell. If you do good things your mind is relaxed. It's as easy as that.

The Buddha said, you should not do things which cause harm to others. Killing or committing suicide are harmful actions. You should not take what has not been given to you. Your sexuality should not do harm to others.

In ancient Japan, killing and suicide were treated differently than they are today. There is an impressive story from the 18th century which is called the 47 Ronin (Mitford, 2005).[8]

When a Daimo (a feudal lord) died, the Samurai under his command became leaderless and were called Ronin. In the 18th century, Kira killed the Daimo Asano with a trick. Kira treated him in such a bad way that Asano wounded Kira with his dagger. As this was forbidden, he was sentenced to death. Three hundred Samurais of Asano became Ronin. And forty-seven of them planned revenge for over two years. Finally, they attacked Kiro's castle and

---

[8]A. B. Mitford reported this event in 1871. His excellent book is still in print and can also be found on Google Books.

killed many of his men and finally him. The Bushido[9] recommended this action, but the Shogunate prohibited revenge of that kind and so the Ronins were sentenced to commit suicide. They did know what was expected and executed themselves and that is the end of the story. In Japan the 47 Ronin became famous for their loyalty and are idols to many.

From their point of view, they did the right action. As the legend says, they were not afraid of their suicidal death. They kept a calm mood, even in the final moment. If one of them would not have been convinced of his actions, he would have had an unsound state of mind. Even apart from what Buddha originally meant, doing the right action makes sense.

In a software project we need to do the right action all the time.

We work with our mind every day and, from an intellectual property point of view, it is sometimes very difficult to tell exactly who brought up a specific idea. It is also easy to extract some files from a huge code base, modify it, and put it on GitHub or Bitbucket.

Sometimes we need to utilize social networks for our work, but it's rare. Let's think about social networks as our free time, and then browsing through them becomes stealing working time. It's just a few minutes, right? One argument for browsing social networks is to relax the mind between two heavy programming tasks. While it is true

---

[9]Bushido was the rule Japanese warriors lived by. It implied a strict moral code.

that we are not coding machines, it is certainly not the right action to browse social networks. It is like overloading an overloaded brain. A walk through the office building or staring out of the window is way more relaxing and beneficial to you and your employer.

Sexual harrassment is a serious issue in companies. There is no need to elaborate on it further than to just say: stay away from it.

Right action summarizes basically what is often called the "Code of Conduct" in many companies. It's there to protect people from being harmed by other people. Hurting others is not good at all. That's why you should act right.

Right Livelihood

One should live in a way which does not do harm to other beings. Working as a butcher or worker in meat production, selling alcohol, drugs, slaves, or animals is doing harm, so is dealing with weapons.

Sounds like we are fine as programmers for now. But please don't forget that you probably work for companies dealing with weapons, selling alcohol, or meat products on their online shop. If you want to become a Buddhist one day, you need to reconsider the customers you work for. These days it is pretty easy to earn money with the wrong things.

The readers of this book are most likely not Buddhists, but only interested in another programmer's view on Zen. The good thing is, in Zen you have to justify your actions for yourself, and the Buddha's recommendations are not the Ten Commandments.

Still, a programmer should only work on software projects which conform with his personal ethics. If you feel doubt about a software project, you shouldn't do it. Luckily in the rich countries of this earth it is pretty easy for most programmers to say "no", because it is so easy to get a new job. It is more difficult in poor countries or in collective societies. In the first one you are glad to have a job and need the money. In the second one the whole society puts pressure on you and you might not have a choice.

I am in the lucky situation to live in a rich country where I have opportunity to say "no" and have already done so in the past. I refuse to work for nuclear energy companies and companies which are known to harm the environment. I am also strict on saying "no" to military companies. But I am happy to help my friend with his website, which imports cider to my country, even though it is not recommended to drink alcohol from a Buddhist point of view.

Many times you alone decide to accept your project or not. Sometimes you can grab a few kilos of rice and move on. Sometimes you can't and need to deal with the situation. Even Zen-Master Kôdô Sawaki had such a problem, when he was forced to serve in the military during the Russian-Japanese war.

That said, think twice before you accept projects which do not conform to your ethics. If you believe you need the money, please be aware that in the long term you are selling happiness. With taking money from projects which you consider unethical, you'll finally feed the fires of your personal hell.

Right Effort

Energies in your mind may lead to aggression, frustration, violence, and so on. The Eightfold Path says we should put effort in raising and maintaining wholesome states of mind. We should abandon or prevent negative states. In other words: think differently. You decide if your day is going to be a good one or a bad one.

A mind can easily become a negative state. It is Jon's boss who forgot that Jon was a junior programmer and straight from university. Maybe he accuses Jon for things somebody else did. Before the situation clears up, Jon's boss is gone, leaving him with a lot of things he needs to deal with.

Jon could spend the remaining hours of his workday with anger and frustration. Finally he could go home and tell his wife about what happened. Even with a lot of beer, his evening is completely lost and his dreams are awful.

Or he could have started laughing when his boss left. Actually the error is on his boss's side, not his. His boss failed to understand the situation before screaming. It was unfair and, if Jon could lose his job because of that, it is like a bad joke.

Laughing would help him to come back into a more positive mind state. There is nothing he could do in this situation. Why should he waste even more valuable time with it? Even worse, Jon's wife could also become angry.

If Jon had kids, they would recognize something is wrong. There is no need to take your boss more seriously than that: it is a sad story about a man who totally lost control.

Do you remember the story about Mike showing Paul his new cell? When Paul recognizes how urgently he wants to have that phone, he should sit back, take a breath and try to control his rising emotions. No need to get this phone— just try to get out of believing that you need it.

Right Effort means you try to keep control of your mind.

Right Mindfulness

Having the right mindfulness helps you to recognize what your body, mind, feelings, and the things surrounding you tell. It is a little bit of what psychologists call "introspection" nowadays. The ability to look into yourself and see things clearly as much as possible. When you listen to yourself you are able to overcome not only desires but also other problems.

As programmers we are often forced to work overtime. Maybe the client has found a bug in production which costs thousands or even millions of dollars every hour. Or the planned release of the new version of your software service cannot happen, which causes terrible problems in the marketing division. Or there is just a low budget for the project. Sometimes we work for low budgets and do overtime at night, but need to be free again after a specific amount of days. It is not a good way to live and work, but sometimes it is necessary.

You can work under high pressure for a long while; but there will be a time when you will become tired. You need to recognize that feeling when it appears and treat it with respect. Your body is telling you to shutdown your brain and get some rest. Of course you can overcome your bodies signals for a while which ultimately leads to sickness, depression or even death. In Japan there is even a word for "death by work". It is Karoshi (Jap.: 過労死). There is a lot of hard work waiting for you in Zen monasteries too. But it is of a different kind, more balanced. It is true that you get up early; but you don't need to work in hectic and stressful environments from 6am to 10pm. Monks concentrate while eating, while meditating, and even while going to the bathroom. Managers usually have a business lunch, do powerlearning sometimes when sleeping,[10] and answer text messages from their cells straight from the bathroom. Non-balanced people sometimes ignore their body even when it responds with neurodermatitis, tinnitus, or constant headache.

Right Mindfulness means you are aware of your desires and emotions. Being aware of yourself—body and mind—helps a lot to keep yourself in a good state of mind.

---

[10]Powerlearning is a method to learn while you are asleep. You play a teaching audio track when you are going to bed and the next day it seems you have learned something. I have never actually tried it and cannot tell if it works or not.

Right Concentration

Our mind is easily distracted. Sometimes we go to work and put the computer on with the intention to work quickly and efficiently and leave the office early. The first email with the latest news from the technology world is often enough to change our plans. Then there is instant messaging, the daily cup of coffee, and a nice chat with a colleague. At 10am you can finally start, but then you daydream about the nearby beach. After all that you stay in the office until 8pm to catch up with the work.

Buddhism's right concentration is actually not referring to concentrated work. It's referring to meditation. In meditation you mostly concentrate on your breath. More advanced students do not even need to concentrate on breathing. In martial arts and other Japanese arts it is all about the breath and the right Ki. When you practice meditation the right concentration will come on its own—sometimes throughout the day. It will help you to focus your mind and this will make it free, giving you rest and peace. It is the goal of many to keep this even-minded state in every situation of your life.

With the right concentration you'll be able to think set priorities better. You can move out the incoming newsletter from your mind. It can wait until tomorrow. Instant messages seem to constantly knock on your brain, waiting for an instant response. But we are not machines. As programmers we have a valuable asset: our concentration. We cannot let it go for free. People need to wait until you have the time to respond to such messages.

Right concentration helps you to efficiently get your work done and enjoy the much deserved evening on the beach. Even there it is helpful: you deserve the beach, and no work will distract you. Lying on the beach can be a good practice too.

For me, meditation practice is very important. Honestly, it saved me. It put my feet back on earth when I was about to burn out. Kôdô Sawaki, was much happier than I, without any money yet still working very hard. He had a good life and emphasized the importance of meditation (Zazen) his whole life.

I started seriously with meditation because of him. I was not sure what I should expect from it. I just started and that was probably the best thing I could do. Expecting anything from meditation is the wrong approach. Just do it.

With meditation you are training the right concentration. While it looks like fun, it is actually very hard work. Especially if you go to a retreat and meditate for three whole days in a row, you will find out how exhausting meditation can be. With meditation you reject the trash of the day and return to planet earth. You quit daily business. It sets you at a distance from the "you as the worker" and brings you back to the "you as a human". Many top managers practice meditation. Guess why?

Why Zen Programming?

Zen is a serious thing. It can be a life changer. But it will only change as much as you want it to change. I call people who are pragmatic, realistic, and with both feet on the earth "Zen Programmers". Even when the world turns upside down, they are still reliable and friendly. It has basically nothing to do with their actual religion. It's the way they behave. The goal of this book is to help you get your feet back on earth too.

To change the way you think is not a trivial job. It's the work of a whole life. I am still practicing this myself and I am far from saying: "I have reached the goal." If you are thinking about the goal, you are missing the way. See the goal as part of the way. Sometimes you lose the path, but you'll come back to it. Don't try to be a perfect wanderer. Just try to follow the way, but don't expect anything.

The question remains. Why should you walk this way? If you are in doubt, this chapter will give you an idea of what can go wrong and why you should search for something different.

The Things We Have to Deal With

What makes a project worse? When do we go home and think, "heck, I need to get out of this"? The following is a list of things programmers will face from time to time. They make us tired and exhausted. Most likely there is no chance to avoid them, we have to deal with them somehow.

The Wrong Team

If you are on the wrong team, you have a problem. Maybe they are all nice, but when one of your team is unhappy with the money or bored by trivial tasks he can ruin the atmosphere. Others might look only at their own career, which makes them very bad team partners. You help them to reach their own goals. Unfriendly situations may arise if a team member has too little knowledge. You might also be in trouble if you have taken a job which just doesn't fit your skill set or where there is nobody who can help you with your first steps.

Teams need to be balanced. If you have the luck to be on a team where "the team shares one dream", everything can be great. If you are part of a team consisting of bored or egotistical people, you can have a pretty tough time.

Grotesque Requirements

Some requirements read more like a science fiction novel and are far from being concrete or realistic. It is fine to have a vision. But the vision needs to fit the team. If you have fresh graduates in an engineering team, it is very unlikely you will build the best cloud-based spreadsheet of all time with the first release.

Some customers tend to think requirements can be outlined with just one sentence: "the product must be like social network X, just a little different." "Things can't be so difficult" when other companies provide them for free. "It's just a message board"—requirements lead to high dissatisfaction. The customer never gets the product of his vision. The developer never manages to satisfy his customer nor does he ever manage to feel competent enough for his job.

Alien Expectations

Not only the lack of requirements leads to alien expectations. Sometimes it seems that people mix up programmers with some kind of superhero.

It is simply not possible to successfully debug a project with 100,000 lines of code when you have just gotten access to it. Be it a production problem or not, programmers usually need the time to read the code before they can fix anything on it.

Phrases like "it is just a button" or "the old programmer did things like that in five minutes" do not help. That aside, the five-minute-fixes might be the root cause for the fixes.

The Night Below the Coffee Machine

Sometimes it is necessary to go beyond the limits and just try to get things done. Assuming a total software failure in production, we need to save what can be saved. It often requires extra overtime, working half of the night or longer.

Software problems are so critical that programmers are expected to stay until the issues are gone. The best of us were found sleeping below the coffee machine, desperately trying to stay awake—but finally failing. Sleeping below the coffee machine shows our commitment to the project in the eyes of some.

While it is sometimes fun to live like that, it becomes a serious problem when you do that on a regular basis. It is even worse if you "fix" the problems of mismanagement. When the requirements are broken or the project management promises a deadline because of politicial reasons it can be a very frustrating experience to stay away from your own family, bed, and home.

Not Dealing with Life

Programmers create bugs. It is normal. You cannot prevent them. Psychologists found out that people can think about three things at the same time pretty easily. If the number goes above three, most of us have problems. As programmers we have to remember many more things at once.

There are a lot of distractions surrounding programmers, like:

- shouting project managers
- constant calls and meetings
- working under pressure
- or simply our family, health, or finances.

So the more distractions a programmer has, the higher the likeliness that he writes buggy code. While a few distractions can be kept at a minimum, others are just there and can't be influenced. Family life, for example, is an important aspect of our lives, even though it can be pretty tough sometimes.

Whoever calculates the budget of a project needs to schedule some extra time for non-work life. Numbers should not be based on working experience alone. They need to take into account a person's current situation. To calculate properly, one needs to know whether someone has a pregnant wife at home, whether they are healthy again, or whether they already recovered from the exhausting project.

Ignoring our lives means we ignore taking risks or chances.

Filling up an energized person with boring tasks means you miss a chance. Giving highly complex tasks to somebody whose family is ill increases your risk.

Seeing your life constantly ignored is frustrating and tiring.

Motivation By Threats

Threats are surely not a good motivational strategy. Still they are used. "If you can't manage to do more overtime, you simply are not good enough at being a programmer and should become a gardener," a colleague of mine once said.

Threats cause fear. One of the strongest fears of humans—besides the fear of the dark—is the fear of losing the grounding for their existence.

If one faces a threat for a while and works in fear, he is definitely one of the best candidates for "burn out".

Changing Requirements

"Management by helicopter" happens when a project manager enters the room, throws in new requirements and leaves. It's like landing, raising dust, and taking off again. A couple of people excel at this. Most of the requirements are not well thought out and, in the middle of the implementation, things might change without prior warning.

When the requirements are not clear, there is no goal and the end of a task cannot be reached. Every meeting becomes absurd and all discussed outcome is nonsense. Finally, the whole project can be doubted and the sense of what one does each day is questioned.

Greed

In a modern society you need money to survive. At least, if you have decided not to live as a monk.

In some occasions, companies—or, well, let us say the managers of companies—squeeze out every dollar of a project without looking at their employees.

In 2012 there was a protest movement at Foxconn China. Workers said they would commit suicide if their working conditions did not change. Apple cooperated with Foxconn. It is said the employees did not even have access to water while working.

In Western countries it is likely that you will have

access to water. Still you might be forced to always stay at the cheapest hotel, take the cheapest transportation, and use the cheapest equipment possible. Even when your project is highly successful and profitable. Saving money on employees while demonstrating how profitable the company is may be the worst error management can do. I have seen a lot of people leave a company because of that.

More Prejudice

I could write an entire book just on things which make programmers frustrated. In this chapter we have looked at a few on them.

Here are a few more prejudices, which you might have heard of already:

Great programmers ...

- can code in language X, if they can code in language Y.
- can fix issues quickly, most of them in under a minute.
- do not write faulty code.
- do not need to write test code.
- love to write code for their customers even late at night.
- can debug code when they are not on a computer or in the office.
- know everything about hardware, recent trends, frameworks, etc. "Everything" actually means everything.

- can understand what a customer means without speaking to him.
- can understand all operating systems from the bottom up, including each and every mobile device.
- can write code which runs on every device without recompiling, device switches, or any additional effort.

The list of prejudice-based expectations is endless. We can't teach people to stop believing things like that. Even professional organizations fail at it. Instead we need to defend ourselves from these expectations on a daily basis.

Burnout

The "burnout" syndrome is something which is often discussed in Germany at the time of this writing. Basically it describes some kind of breakdown because of overworking, boredom, or a similar reason. If you suffer from it, you are out of energy in a way healthy people cannot imagine. It leads to depression and in some extreme cases can cause suicide. Diagnosis is difficult and for that reason some people claim that burnout does not exist.

Does Burnout Actually Exist?

Some say people, who complain about burnout, are just lazy, but certainly not sick. They compare it to situations they had years before and—surprise—years they had worked a similar amount of hours and had never heard of something like burnout.

Others feel exhausted and need a vacation. When they have an intense phase of working, they call the exhaustion a burnout. Sometimes only because they are too tired to go out for a beer.

There are some people who I consider to really be burned out. If you were one of that group, you would most likely not have any energy or time to speak about your problems. You would be more worried about surviving the day. A few who have managed to get out of this misery have written books about that time. It must have been a horrible experience.

As mentioned, burnout diagnosis is difficult. How can medical staff separate exhaustion from burnout? The latter is considered a disease of the mind—how can you differ it from other diseases? Depressive behavior and other symptoms do not necessary come from a burnout, even when one is working hard. Actually we cannot decide for sure if you get it or not. If it is caused by bacteria, it would be possible. But like this? That's surely a reason why it is discredited. Misusing the term in day-to-day talks is perhaps another reason.

I would also like to point to the DSM-V. This is the "Diagnostic and Statistical Manual of Mental Disorders" published by the American Psychiatric Association (APA). Basically it is a classification system to diagnose things like ADHD or binge eating. It is noteworthy that the burnout syndrome still doesn't have a diagnosis. In other terms, there is no standard way to identify a burnout syndrome. While I am no expert, you might want to know that I strongly believe burnout is an existing disease. I got this opinion because I started to study psychology in addition to my job and became interested in the psychology of work in general. There is a lot of literature about the topic. Some of them are on a scientific level and these are the ones you should read if you would like to learn more.

The Ultimate List of How to Feel Burned Out

Burnout is not restricted to top managers. Everybody can get it. There are documented cases of shepherds with burnout from watching sheep eating grass for twenty years. What they get is "**burn**out", but the press often refers to it as "**bore**out".

As a software programmer there are many options, many of them are tied to the things which were mentioned before.

Matthias Burisch is a German scientist who wrote a great book on burnout syndrome (Burisch, 2006). He is very popular for his research and shows that burnout is rooted in irregular working times, instant availability, pressing dead-lines, and competition. While this sounds pretty familiar to anybody who has worked as a programmer, he actually researched across all occupation groups.

He also mentioned that there are people who work in exhausting environments and do not suffer from burnout syndrome. For example, nurses working in intensive care units are not so much in danger as nurses working somewhere else. Why is there a difference?

Burisch reasoned burnout is a very complex syndrome which combines multiple factors. Not every stressful situation guarantees burnout. Everybody handles situations differently. One programmer might suffer, but another could handle the situation without any further problems. In this case the second programmer might be tempted to think that the first is simply not strong enough. This is a wrong conclusion, as it might have just been a problem with the combination of factors. Besides the general problematic situation for the first programmer, social pressure might also arise.

The factors which might lead to burnout according to Burisch are:

- work overload
- loss of control
- little or no reward
- breakdown of common sense
- little or no equity
- ethical conflicts

We have spoken about a lot of these factors already.

Facts?

Ignoring that times changed is a common reaction of IT managers when discussing burnout syndrome. "I worked a similar amount of hours when I was young," some say.

"They are just lazy," others say. In Germany, some IT managers point out other countries and explain nobody there is suffering from this disease, so it must be a fiction.

Can we really compare country X with country Z when it comes to things like that? In Germany there is a great healthcare system and enough food and water for everybody. One of the biggest problems is the weather which becomes worse every year. In Africa there are different problems. There is hunger. There are not so many jobs. There isn't even always access to clean water. When you need to find water, you probably do not care much about something like burnout syndrome.

A couple of years ago there was a headline in a German newspaper: "Has Japan burned out?" The authors mentioned that Japanese people are burning out more and more. My assumption is now that rich countries with a high industrialization standard have more time and resources to deal with the disease, or even to identify it. It doesn't mean it is nonexistent in other countries. I will stick with Germany.

Focus is a magazine in Germany. It's pretty huge and reaches lots of people. They published a few interesting statistics (Gebert, 2010). In 1993 around 30% of the causes of being disabled were because of musculoskeletal disorders. In 2008 it dropped to only 15%. Instead psychological diseases increased to 35.6%. These numbers show how today's work has changed in twenty years. A psychologist explained in the same article that our working structures are way more complex than in the past and not everybody is made for that kind of work. Smartphones and other technological gadgets did not exist twenty years ago. These toys are eating up a lot of our time at home. We programmers are always expected to stay up to date with these things and always to be available. We need to learn about different operating systems, different social media tools, and we need to read books on programming. Besides all of that, we need to work for at least forty hours a week. We are flooded by information and our minds can't take a break.

Other papers reported on serial suicides (Kläsgen, 2010, BBC, 2012). At France Télécom over thirty cases of suicide were documented in 2008 and 2009—one per month. The only reason we can get this statistic is because in France suicide is counted as a work accident. In Germany this is not the case and so German numbers are unknown.

The DAK Hamburg health report brought up a few more numbers (DAK, 2010). DAK is a health insurance agency in Germany. Psychological disease is currently the top third reason for sick leave. It's around twenty-five days per sick person. About 7% of the citizens of Hamburg are on sick leave for around five weeks per year because of psychological disease.

The yearly Stressreport from 2012 does not make things look any better (Lohmann-Haislah, 2012). Since 2006 the biggest psychological issues of employees are multitasking (58%), too tight deadlines (52%), and tasks which are too repetitive (50%). Over 44% of the employees said they experience constant distraction.

Five Phases of Burnout

Work/life balance is not just a phrase. You need to keep yourself healthy and have responsibility for your team when you are a team leader. Sick leave costs you a lot of money and time.

If …

- your work is the central aspect in life,
- you distance yourself from others,
- you become cynical,
- you get into conflicts with people,
- you suffer from depression,

you should be careful. This list is known as the five phases of burnout. If you hear that your colleague has suddenly stopped playing football or doesn't go out any more, you should be worried about him.

You Live Alone, You Die Alone

We can try to exchange our thoughts but how can we be sure that our listener understands what we are trying to express?

Understanding is tied to the context of the current situation and the context in which we live. In addition, our thinking itself differs. It makes it impossible to exchange our ideas like we exchange emails—in programming terms, we have no common format. When I say "apple", the image in my mind cannot be the same as the one you have in your mind. Even when I paint the image it does not look like my initial thought. Even if I could, your perception would not be the same as the perception I have of the same image. This is because perception is also tied to the context and to your own experience. That all being said, there is nobody who is actually like you or I. We can try to express but nobody can understand exactly. That's why we live alone. You will die alone. You might have many friends and you might be a rich person. But after all that you will die alone. Nobody can accompany you. Nobody can change seats with you. Kôdô Sawaki once said, you cannot even exchange a fart. And finally when the moment of our death comes and we leave this world, nobody can join us. We need to do it alone.

The only permanent thing in life is that there is no permanence. Everything is in flow, like water. But it is no reason to grieve. If we understand this, we can also understand that in our life it is all about us. We can not live for anybody else. It is our own life which we can't exchange or share.

> No matter what happens to you—it is your life.
>
> —Kôdô Sawaki (Sawaki, 2008)

Once we have understood this truth we can live freely

and without sorrow and grief. If we have an accident in which we lose an arm or our legs we might be worried. But it is our life and we have to deal with it. Even without legs we can have a good life. It is just a matter of viewpoint.

When we get a job which causes us grief, it is our life. There is no reason to stop living and fall into sorrow and despair. Zen practice helps us to see the things a bit more like how they actually are. Zen helps us find our true nature and with that we can accept the things which happen to us more easily.

Kizen and Other Practices

Introduction

This chapter is about how you can get your feet back on earth. It is a collection of techniques you can apply right now. There are not only "Japanese" ideas here, but actually a lot more things from all over the world which I think are useful for keeping a Zen mind.

You are probably reading this because you feel that you have lost contact with the real world. Most likely it's like that because work controls you and has become omnipresent in many or most aspects of your life.

We often forget that we all are just humans. We forget that we need food, rest, and sometimes even nice warm words to feel comfortable. We forget that the same things are true for the guy on the other side of the table. With the following practices I have relearned how to be aware of these things.

Zen is not theory. Zen is practice—with body and mind.

Look at the Kōan (Jap.: 公案) practice. A Kōan is a riddle given by Zen master to their students which cannot be solved by rational thinking. A Kōan shows Zen can not be understood with a rational mind. One of the most well-known Kōan is:

Two hands clap and there is a sound. What is
the sound of one hand?

This Kōan is attributed to Hakuin Ekaku, a influential
person to the Rinzai school. There are multiple answers.
One of them is:

Om.

If you would give this answer to your Zen master, he
most likely would not accept it. You would need to find
your own answer. It happens that monks try to find a
solution for their Kōan for years.

As a Shakuhachi (bamboo flute) player, my tone is
my Kōan. There is no answer in playing. I can't even say
practice alone would make the right tone. I could blow for
ten thousand hours but not find the tone. My Kōan will
never end.

From books alone, one will not master Zen. With this
thought in mind, I searched for ways to keep my mind in a
good condition and practice Zen even in the office.

Ki 気: Breath and Vitality

All of the Japanese arts I am aware of have one thing in
common: they use Ki (Jap.: 気). This includes martial arts.
Ki is a term from Daoism and means energy or breath.
When you practice it is said you strengthen your Ki. While
Ki is discussed more often in some arts than in others, all
of them have Ki as their foundation.

Once I sat down with a few Japanese friends to a meal of a couple of bowls of rice and vegetables. We all got chopsticks. Then the rice bowl was passed around and everybody took what he would eat. I was not very used to chopsticks and struggled hard to get rice out of the bowl. Finally, we all laughed about my attempts to eat dinner and our host said: "You must take the rice with Ki! Breathe, as if you were meditating!"

Breathing: without breath we are dead. That's it. Still, we rarely think about how we breathe. We use short breaths in our daily life, just scratching the surface of what we could do with our lungs. A few extraordinary people can dive up to nine minutes and up to 214 meters deep (702 feet). Google Herbert Nitsch. What do we learn from the free divers? It is possible to influence your breath. Not only that, but free diving can also influence heart rate and other bodily functions through its focus on breathing.

Breathing does not only help free divers. When I start to feel stressed because of an insane workload or ridiculous bugs, I think of my bowl of rice. No need for cursing, laughing, or panic. I breathe. I try to be aware of my breath. My breath strengthens my Ki. And with Ki it is possible to pull out the rice without further trouble. With a good Ki it is also possible to find more software errors and stay calm when you fix production bugs while your customer shouts at you.

But let's be honest. Ki might be explained without any metaphysics. Breathing reduces the stress and increases concentration. The moment with a strong Ki—maybe it is simply the moment when your heart stops racing, oxygen floods your brain and your hands stop shaking. However you explain Ki—with a generic approach or with a biological approach, it is a good thing to achieve.

Kizen 記禅: The Way of Code

While Ki is a conceptual way, Kizen (Jap.: 記禅) is a practical way. For example, Suizen describes the way of Shakuhachi playing. Zazen is the way of sitting meditation. After a lot of research I decided to use Kizen as "The way of the code".[11]

Describing Ki with the characters 記禅, does not tie it to just breath or energy, it also has the meaning of writing code, sign, notation, and so on. Also the Kanji implies "action". You pronounce it like the English word "key".

For me, Kizen expresses exactly what we want: the way of the code or the way of the symbols.

Chaos and Rational Thinking

This might happen when your thoughts jump from task to task:

A programmer, let's call him Mike, comes to the office and gets a cup of coffee or tea. He starts the computer and sits at his desk. He makes a plan for today and starts reading

---

[11]My special thanks goes to Mino Suzuki from London, who was so kind and friendly to reply to an email from a complete stranger. She helped me without anything in return. Also thank you to Kiku Day, who put me into contact with Mino Suzuki.

some APIs. After a couple of minutes he remembers an email conversation from yesterday and opens his email client. While he types an answer, his mind jumps to Twitter and he takes a second to open the client. He wants to return quickly to his email, but he finds some interesting news stories. He clicks a few links, reads a couple of webpages, and finally remembers his email. Now, since he is already on Twitter, he decides to read all his Twitter news first. After a couple more websites, he forces himself to do some real work and gets back to his email. He is already angry at himself since he lost quite a bit time. Finally, he comes back to some code and comes up with a great idea, but then remembers that he has an unnecessary meeting. By the time Mike comes back to his desk, it's almost lunch time. His compiler gives him errors and he doesn't really remember what he was doing before he left for the meeting.

The Natural Order

The natural order of thoughts is associative and chaotic. I believe our mind acts as a network. Thoughts cause new thoughts. If you think about an apple, you might also think about apple juice which might remind you of a drink you had recently, which contained apple juice. And this might remind you of a bad hangover.

Sigmund Freud, a psychologist from the 20th century, used this behavior of the mind for treatment. He called it "free association". His patients would sit on a couch and tell him what came into their mind. Freud interpreted the associations.

More modern theories call this way of thinking "network". We have no control over this network. It acts without us, but can be influenced from us with thinking.

Without our senses and nerves, thinking might be associative only. We would need to "close" the input channels from eyes, ears, skin, nose, mouth, and, yes, even cut the nerves from internal organs to achieve pure associative thinking. This is not possible. I call influences from the outside "random events". They cannot be controlled and the effects they have are too complex to calculate. Even when there *might* be a chance to understand this complexity, from today's standpoint they just look chaotic.

This natural order has a high energy cost. Maybe there was once a time where the natural order alone was the best order for us. Maybe even today it is so.

If you are reading a book in the jungle you might be very focused. But if tiger sneaks up on you, it'd be better if you heard the cracking wood. The natural order would wake you up, you would look for the source of the sound and finally spot the tiger. This is very good in the jungle, but bad in the office. If you are writing code and somebody's pen falls down on the floor, you usually don't need to look for the source.

At work, we have different tigers that want to eat us; social networks interrupting our associative thinking with chaos.

Kizen Means Focus

Kizen means to focus on associative thinking and reduce the level of chaos. We need to increase the rational level of our thinking. Chaos and rational thinking must be in balance; rationality is not everything. Chaos is also tied to creativity. I think small portions of chaos might be beneficial for your work.

Work is now. Even if you want to have a little chaos, you can safely shut out most distractions. Software programmers have a difficult job. You are also responsible for the outcome and its quality. When you work you have no time for anything else. Be aware of what you are doing. Stick to those things, don't jump around, not even for a second.

"Reading emails" is often a chaos-driven task. People look at emails when they have a second, see something blinking, or when they are just bored. For a long time I associated boredom with checking my email.

Thinking in Slots

Today I have a couple of fixed slots in my daily plan. The fixed slots are allowed to consume 20% of my time. "Email" is one of them. 20% more of my time is for unexpected things. 60% is reserved for actual work. You could say I calculate around five hours of actual work (given an eight hour workday). You might think this is not a lot, but it is. I tracked my time with Time & Bill[12] after I launched it. I

---

[12]http://www.timeandbill.de

got to a level where I tracked my email time (among other things, like Twitter). I was extremely frustrated when I saw how much *less* I worked each day. On bad days I managed two hours of real work.

I talked to a lot of people about this and found out many had similar experiences. Though of course this is not a representative study. Be honest: does it feel sometimes like you have managed to get simply *nothing* done? Welcome to the club.

Another thing I found out about my working behavior was that my work time was highly fragmented. Sometimes I just worked a couple of minutes on a task. I call it "microslots". I changed this too: microslots simply consume too much energy.

Today I check my email twice a day. Social networks are for after work. When I am coding a complicated part of the software I do not answer phone calls, read SMS or do anything else. There is just one exception: my wife is allowed to call me at any time.

For me slots with a length of thirty to sixty minutes are perfect. After sixty minutes, I am usually tired and need to do something else. When I stop before thirty minutes is up the task becomes simply too taxing on my energy level and creates a lot of garbage in my mind. My numbers are highly dependent on my daily needs and I am not strict about them. You need to figure out your best slot lengths for yourself.

Many programming tasks are too big to be completed in only one day. Often you can break down the job so that it fits into smaller slots, like forty-five minutes.

Mind Garbage Collection

I already mentioned that many small tasks mess with my mind. For example, if you do ten different tasks in half an hour, you already have ten thoughts in your mind, which might create even more tangental thoughts. If you have only one task you focus on, you have just this thought and only a few tangents to deal with.

To clear your mind it is often necessary to reflect on your thoughts. Make sure everything is done well. With ten things in mind, reflection is not so easy.

Reflection is also necessary to make sure the outcome of your work is of good quality. With too many things to think about you'll miss errors. You know that this is true and, with the knowledge that you might have missed something, it is even more difficult to clear up your mind.

You are probably familiar with this situation. Is it the same if you have one problem or five at the same time? When I go to bed with just one big problem, I might sleep badly but at some point I can just say, "Deal with that tomorrow." With five problems I have no control any more. My thoughts go in circles and my night is horrible.

This alone makes it worth it for me to reduce the number of tasks to a level I can handle and which keep me in balance. Some people don't care much about their balance; they enjoy the adrenaline which floods their brains when dealing with a lot of things. I have not met any adrenaline-loving people who really could reflect on their tasks or who were in balance.

You Are Not an Email Machine

If you are a classic programmer, email communication
is not your primary discipline even if half of the world
thinks so. Your main discipline is code, testing, and solving
technical problems. Whenever you have tasks which are
not tied to your core discipline you need to treat them as
secondary and put them in a fixed slot.

Since fixed slots have only limited time, it would mean
you also have to limit your time spent with emails. If you
feel bad when you have just two thirty-minute slots for
your emails, you are either not a full time programmer or
you have a priority problem.

If you practice a Zen way, you need to take it seriously.
Often Zen practice consists of an obviously easy task,
carried out with full concentration and the highest possible
precision. In Zen archery, shooting with a bow can be a
trivial task. Take the arrow, take the bow, shoot. In Zen,
there exist books which explain the right way of thinking,
the right way of breathing, the right way of condition.

Doing something the Zen way means you concentrate
on its core. No distractions. When you are doing Zen
archery, you are the bow. You are the arrow. You are the
wind. You are yourself. There is simply no time to write an
email somewhere in between.

Why do we not treat programming similarly?

When we code, we code. For some reason we are expected to return emails in minutes. If we want to seriously

write code, we need to do it as well as we can. Otherwise we'll never be able to become great programmers in future. If you are a programmer, you are a programmer. Real programmers are still programmers when they eat lunch or travel through the wilderness on their weekends. If we want to live that way, we need to take our skills and our passion seriously. Emails are part of our working day, but not the most important. Therefore they need to reside outside the core of our working day to make room for what is important to us.

There is a "natural time" to work with emails. For me it is most often at the beginning of my day, while drinking my morning coffee. It helps me get in the mood for my real work. Depending on my task, I have a second slot reserved for emails after lunch or before I leave for home. That is enough. Exceeding the time for fixed slots should not happen.

Focus Time

Some others will hate you when you focus. Why? You don't have much time any more for their problems. When they show up at your desk with a question you will not respond immediately. In some cases they might not even be able to continue their own work. But if you help, your own work will be interrupted, putting extra pressure on you. Of course, if you don't help, you cannot expect others to help you when you show up at their desk. Helping each other is not calculated in the usual programming budget—and that's a problem because programmers are expected to be team workers.

If you break the helping-cycle, your colleagues will hate you. You changed the rules of the game and it looks very egoistical if you try to keep a clear mind and focus. Luckily there is a pretty easy way out—just speak with your colleagues.

Try to propose increasing productivity at a team meeting. Define timeframes when you want to focus and timeframes when you are available for discussion. Focus times should never be interrupted except for serious trouble, like server downtimes. One of my focus times is usually 10am to 1pm. I find that I have a good level of energy at this time. These three hours usually mean four or five task slots for me and include a couple minutes' break between them. Having three such productive hours without any distraction make a real difference to me, no matter how bad the rest of the day is.

When you agreed on focus times, don't forget you really need to focus. Tweeting and emailing friends need to be avoided. Otherwise your team will be upset and no longer respects your time. Also don't forget to respect the focus times of others. If others have focus times too, it's a good thing if these times overlap.

Actually focus times work very well with Scrum.[13] The daily meeting could happen after the focus time, when a lot

---

[13]Scrum is a method for developing software. It is a so called agile way to manage software projects because it promises a flexible way of working. It is possible for customers to change their minds even when the project has already started. Communication is very important to make Scrum work. Therefore a short, daily meeting is often held.

of things should have been done. After that meeting, people can discuss questions collected during the focus time.

Pay attention if you have young members in your team. New project members might not have the ability to handle a full period of focus time. Depending on their current level of competence it might make sense to relax the focus rules for them. Once they are fully productive, things are different again.

Chair-Zazen

Zazen is sitting meditation.

In Zen monasteries you sit on a Zafu, which is a small pad, while your knees reside on a Zabuton, some kind of a cushion. You meditate with slightly open eyes to avoid falling asleep. In the Rinzai school you have to solve your Kōan (Jap.: 公案). In the Sōtō school it is preferred to not think at all and to "just sit". This is called Shikantaza (Jap.: 只管打坐). If you want to learn more about the details of Zazen, I recommend you read "Zen Mind, Beginners Mind" from Shunryu Suzuki (Suzuki, 2011).

Zazen is the most important practice in Zen. At work you can't take a Zafu with you. You would need to find a place where you could remain undisturbed. Even if there is such a place, quite a few people would not like to sit full lotus. It is actually very uncomfortable.

One day when I was pretty exhausted from my job as a project manager, I felt like my head was going to explode. Besides, the chaos of a thousand of phone calls and emails awaited me. Not only that, but every second another team member approached my desk with something urgent. I felt the sweat soaking through my shirt. My face was red like a clown's nose and I never knew my heart could manage so many beats per minute. At some point between the calls I had to solve a difficult problem, but couldn't come up with the right thing. I would have to think about it at least for a few minutes. No, even longer—even without a phone I would need to get down from the adrenaline rush.

I needed to calm down. Quickly.

I asked my colleague to take all my phone calls for the next fifteen minutes. A small sign on the door told visitors that I was not able to answer questions until I said otherwise. Then I turned my chair and stared at the wall, where a big clock was hanging. I felt safe and comfortable because nobody could look at me. I tried to sit up straight and observed my breathing. It was a hectic in and out with no control. It took me a few minutes to get back to normal breathing. My heart beat also went back to normal operation. My blood pressure dropped back to normal. I suddenly had a bad headache which I hadn't felt earlier. I accepted it was there and soon it was gone. I sat for around ten minutes, staring at the clock with half-open eyes and observing my breath. My mind was full of work but I tried to focus on my breath. Finally, things slowed down. The next five minutes I sat comfortably, looking through the window. This was the time when I made the decision.

This isn't really Zazen, as it lacks all the formality and philosophy. It is more office meditation—chair zazen. Something we programmers can easily do. I still do this when I feel my work overwhelm me or when I am tired. After ten minutes I get my balance back and can work as quickly as ever.

Many employers I know are fine with you taking time out. The act of programming is not typing alone, it is also thinking, considering, deciding. A lot is done in our minds. Don't be afraid to get your hands off the keyboard and gaze at the wall. Just don't fall asleep or think about your free time—Chair Zazen should be used for meditation, not for joy.

Office-Kinhin

Kinhin is a meditation form which is rather uknown in the Western world, compared to Zazen, the sitting meditation. Kinhin is actually used in combination with Zazen. Kinhin is a walking meditation. Maybe you have seen a couple of monks walking slowly in a row. This is Kinhin.

From time to time, monks and interested people like me attend not only the usual daily meditation practice but also retreats, so called Sesshin (Jap.: 接心). A retreat consists of intense days of concentration. I have been told many days are needed to make the "mind monkey" rest. This is a requirement to see one's own nature. It seems this idea is rooted in Rinzai Zen, but I haven't been able to find a literary source for this.

When I first sat for three days in a row, I felt pain which I never thought was possible. My legs hurt and on the last day it was hard to concentrate on practice rather than on my hurting legs. Between the sitting periods, which were usually up to thirty minutes, Kinhin practice is recommended. It relaxes the feet and keeps you in concentration. I learned to love it.

These days I practice Kinhin in the office. Especially when I have a longer focus time to do it between time slots. It doesn't take long, but it helps me when I lose concentration, when I am tired, or when I feel like my head is going to explode. In summertime I go out and breathe some fresh air.

If you would like to start with it too, I recommend you to choose a good route. A good route is one which does not require a lot of cognitive work to traverse: few traffic lights, not too many dangerous streets to pass. Also avoid noisy places and places with a lot of people. If possible, a nearby park with trees, birds, and maybe a little water would be perfect. I also used the hall or the hallway of my company. It is important that you can just walk without distraction and without speaking to anybody. The environment does not need to be beautiful, but it helps.

While you can do Kinhin as long as you want, twenty minutes is a great time for a longer walk. When time is short, I also walk for only a few minutes—it helps too.

When walking, look at the floor. Go slowly and concentrate on your breath. Let it flow, without rushing or slowing down too much. Breathe naturally. For me, a full breathing cycle takes me four steps.

Once you have managed to breathe accordingly, you can try to be aware of your feet. Breathe and feel how your heel touches the earth, how the ball goes down and finally your toes finish the movement. Walk, do not think. Let coding problems and business trouble go for these few minutes of Kinhin you have. Just walk.

Sleep

Is Napping Dumb?

The artist Salvador Dali invented something he called "slumber with a key". One afternoon, when he became tired, he took a key in his hand and sat into a chair to take a nap. Once the key fell down, the sudden noise woke him. He said, his "physical and psychic" being were being revived. Albert Einstein is said to have taken similar naps.

If the internet doesn't lie, many famous people were known to nap regularly.

Winston Churchill was a napper. He actually had his own bed in the House of Parliament. He thought napping was the key to his success in the second world war.

Napoleon, John F. Kennedy, Ronald Reagan, and Thomas Edison took naps often. You can read about it on the web[14].

Sleep is something essential. I heard that in the sixties some people hoped modern technology would release us from hard work and make us a community of consumers. We seem, however, to work even more these days. With the arrival of smartphones and tablets, we work any time, any place. We work even when we are so tired that we cannot think anymore. To help us back in the saddle, we

---

[14]http://artofmanliness.com/2011/03/14/the-napping-habits-of-8-famous-men

drink coffee. I hear people say: "Wow, I am already tired again, just after six hours of work!" Can we refuse to accept that we get tired after a couple of hours? Why do we rate work and many other things, like computer gaming, higher than one of the most essential things in our life?

I have never seen a colleague napping in the office. Not sure why—maybe it is because others would point their fingers at him and call him lazy. Maybe it makes us look "weak". I don't know but, with Dali, Einstein, and Churchill in mind, I definitely would not think badly of others napping in the office.

Let's face it: there are often other groups of people who have incredible power over us. Their names are Customers, Bosses, and Colleagues. We call ourselves "free people" or "individualists"—but we don't have the freedom to take a nap when our bodies need and deserve it.

How sad.

Sleep When You Are Tired

Lin-Ji once said (LUC, 2013):

> Defecate, urinate, put on clothes, eat food, and lie down when you are tired. Fools may laugh at me, but the wise understand.
>
> —Lin-Ji (around 845 CE)

Lin-Ji was the founder of the Rinzai tradition, a popular but very strict school of Zen. The quote could also be rephrased as: "Sleep when you are tired. Eat when you are hungry." It is so easy. All the most famous people in history slept when they were tired. Why shouldn't you? You could eat for just half of your lunch break and spend the rest of the time napping in a lounge. Some big companies provide such a room. Or maybe you can learn to nap in a chair like Dali. Best case scenario you can lock up the office door without being disturbed. A while ago, even before I learned about Zen, I was so tired that I went to my car at lunch time and slept for an hour.

Let us look at ourselves in some kind of Zen-way; we are humans. We do not need much to survive, just a safe home, some food, water, and some kind of clothing to keep us warm. That's all.

In a modern world we think this is not enough. We want a great car, an iPod, and to go out for dinner as often as we want. We consider this lifestyle luxurious and think we have a worse life when we can't get it. To achieve these goals of happiness, we work like maniacs and ignore our body. We sometimes don't eat when we are hungry and we sometimes don't sleep when we need to rest. We cannot, because otherwise we might lose our comfort.

In Zen it is a goal to sleep when tired and eat when hungry. Try to do that. It is difficult. But it should not be— it is the most fundamental thing in our human lives.

The Perfect Nap

The post-lunch feeling—full of food and too tired to work. The only hope was to somehow reach the coffee machine. It hit me regularly and I decided to stop eating lunch. I wasn't tired anymore, just hungry—and the hunger kept me awake.

To be honest, it was not a good idea to live like that. After a while I felt pretty stressed and unhealthy in general. I started to eat small portions for lunch again. My food was reduced, like rice with soy. It helped a little, but still I felt tired in the afternoon. Finally, I started to nap when I felt too tired to work. Often a couple of minutes were enough, like what Dali did. On rare occasions I needed thirty minutes. I didn't rest longer because I wouldn't be able to get back into a normal routine if I did.

I researched a bit about my experiences and learned scientists use EEGs[15] to learn more about sleep itself. With the machine's help, they have divided sleep into five phases.

Phase 1 is the start of the sleep phase. It is very light and muscles start to relax. Dali would lose his key in that phase. Phase 2 brings you to Phases 3 and 4, which we call "deep sleep". Lastly, there is REM sleep. The EEG would write Alpha-, Beta-, Theta- or Delta-Waves after which the first four phases are named. To identify REM sleep you do not really need an EEG. You can tell a person is in REM when their eyeballs are rapidly moving behind their closed eyelids.

---

[15]EEG is short for electroencephalogram. It is a machine which visualizes electric activity of your brain by printing out the waves on paper rolls.

Like Dali, it is best for me to stay in Phase 1. It makes sense: it is often better and more efficient to refresh the browser (my mind) instead of the operating system (my body). Lin-Ji didn't think in EEG-Waves. He most likely did not know as much about sleep as we do today. But he was right when he recommended us to sleep when we are tired.

Sleep Deprivation

You can easily suffer from sleep deprivation in Zen monasteries.

There are a couple of stories where aspiring monks wait for three days in front of the Rinzai monastery for entrance. They do not sleep, they do not sit. They knock on the doors from time to time, just to be thrown down the stairs. If you enter, there is no time to rest: a lot of unwanted jobs are awaiting you. In some monasteries you wake up early at 3:00am or so. Your day is full of hard work and it is not surprising that quite a few fall asleep while meditating.

Why do they not respect Lin-Ji's advice?

Isn't Zen about learning to sleep when you are tired?

In Zen you learn many things. One of the most important is to forget yourself. This is hard practice and is a different way than we laymen go.

Even though the monk's practice is honorable, we have other things to think about, as we have decided not to live a spiritual life. We'll most likely not reach the state of "sleep when tired". It is not easy to achieve that, but we can still make it our goal and find a few good reasons for it.

First, when you are tired you are not efficient. Your boss complains about your nap. Your eyes could be open, but that is not a guarantee you are actually thinking about what you do or that you are coding efficiently.

Second, creativity goes hand in hand with sleep. It has been said that Albert Einstein got his best ideas when he slept around twelve hours. When students prepare for exams it would be best if they nap when they have learned something important. Sleep helps to reorganize the newly collected knowledge. Experiences are being processed, new ideas are arising. Sleep removes bio-waste from the body.

Software is crafted with the mind. This makes it a creative task, even though I would not say software has anything to do with art.

Work Without Holidays

A horse riding instructor I know travels a lot to hold courses. She once said, everybody should work in a way that no holidays are needed.

In Germany we often work from 8am to 5pm. There is less time for privacy, just plain work with only a short lunch break. You work hard and finally can say: "Wow, glad the day is over!" The rest of the day is often consumed by the TV. The best hours of the day have been spent at work, sometimes without passion and without energy. In the evening there is no energy left for anything interesting.

After a couple of months the exhaustion level rises and we "need" the "deserved" break—holidays.

I lived like that for a long time. It made me sick and so

I went to the "sleep when tired" philosophy. Today I work more than ever. I work every day, including Saturdays and Sundays. But I do not feel exhausted nor do I need holidays. My last holiday was over two and a half years ago (at the time of this writing in April 2013).

It happens that I sometimes have no work in the afternoon. Recently, the sun was out after a long, dark winter. I stopped working because I had no pressing deadlines. I went out with my family.

Sometimes I play the Shakuhachi in the afternoon. It refreshes me and is fun. It happens when I am fed up with the tech world.

In other terms: I refuse to work from 8 to 5. It's simply a bad idea. I can decide when to work on my own because I am self employed. Instead I work when I am motivated. Sometimes it is late at night, when I get a good idea for a new feature. Sometimes it is early in the morning, because the birdsongs make me feel comfortable. But I never work when my son needs my attention, when I am out of energy, or when I am tired.

It is not only the best for me and my family. It is also the best for my customer. They simply get the best I can give.

I realized a few things when I changed to that mode:

1. I constantly have a high level of energy.
2. I am very motivated with everything, my family, my job, my spare time.
3. My life feels as if I am on constant vacation.
4. The quality of my work is much higher.

5. My customers are much more satisfied.

Yes, I fail with it sometimes. There are unforseen bugs or other issues which disturb my peaceful life. I still know the word "stress". But the overall situation lets me deal better with stress.

Drink Tea

I drink coffee, lots of it. Maybe too much. Until lunch time, you can always find a cup of coffee on my desk. I drink it while working. It often gets cold, but I don't care. I am fine with cold coffee. On rare occasions my coffee becomes cold before I even taste it. I am used to cold coffee actually.

For me coffee is nothing special.

Have you heard of Cha-do? It translates to the "tea way" and is another Zen practice in which you follow a strict ritual to drink tea.

It is very difficult. You have to follow special rules on how to prepare tea, how to drink tea, and how to clean up. It is an elegant practice.

If you drink coffee like me, then this is very different from Cha-Do. We drink coffee to stay awake, even though it is not healthy at all. We don't pay special attention to coffee.

From time to time I change things up.

Why shouldn't you go out to your office kitchen one or two times a day and prepare coffee (or tea) with special attention to detail? You can make it your own ritual. Buy great coffee beans. Crush them manually and use one of the espresso makers which you need to put on the stove. Prepare foam by hand. It will take you around ten minutes. Take another ten minutes and drink your cup of coffee. Just concentrate on every sip you take. Clean up silently, and take care of every single step you make.

As you know by now, I am a regular coffee drinker. I found out that my "ritual" works better when I drink tea with special attention. It is an extraordinary drink for me, and as an extraordinary event it helps me to get out of routine work. I have learned a lot about tea since I started doing this. I try to make the best tea possible every time I prepare tea.

Don't forget to avoid speaking while you are drinking tea. It is not always possible to remain silent when the kitchen is full of colleagues. If you are disturbed, make it clear that you are making tea. If that doesn't help, interrupt your preparations and concentrate on your colleague. You need full attention for tea, there is not a single thought left for the work you want to escape from.

Clean your dish. This is non-negotiable and part of your ritual. Just as you prepared the cup and filled it with water by hand, you should also clean your dish by hand. Clean it in a way that you can't wait to use it for the next tea ritual.

Clean

Programmers are expected to get work done. We often have a hard time keeping in sync with all of our duties. It eventually leads us to get to our keyboard as early as possible and leave it as late as possible. Every second counts.

In Zen monasteries cleaning up is part of the daily duties. Sometimes it seems to me as if they meditate half of the day and clean up the other half. A clean environment is not only necessary for the kitchen, it is an absolute requirement for the Zen-dō (Jap.: 禅堂).[16] You simply cannot concentrate on your breath when everything is dusty. You cannot hold your eyes in a fixed position when there are a thousand objects lying around.

In the same vein, can you concentrate on coding when your fingers always hit the chocolate between the keys? Can you enjoy your coffee when there are three other cups from the past days around? Isn't a dusty monitor just annoying?

How are we supposed to take care of software if we cannot take care of our desk?

All is connected: mind, body, environment.

You might be able to write good code in a dirty environment. But you'll need extra energy to find the right concentration and mood to complete your job.

With a few minutes everyday we can have a clean desk and a fresh working atmosphere. It is your responsibility alone, not the one of the cleaning lady. Clean up your own dirt. There is no excuse if the cleaning lady is on sick leave.

On your desk are only the things which you need "now". There is nothing which is for "later" or for "never".

Take care of ambience. Your eyes need to relax from

---

[16]The room of meditation. Zen-dō are not only found in monasteries, every room in which Zen is practiced is basically a Zen-dō.

the monitor. You should be able to look through the room without anything catching your attention. Distracting pictures or unopened packing cases are definitely not doing any good. Your office is not a dump. If there is not the right place for an object, it doesn't belong in the office. Your office is your Zen-dō—treat it like that.

Take Breaks: Sesshin

Multiple times a year Zen monks do Sesshin. The doors of monasteries are closed and a time of intense meditation starts. Most of the day the monks sit silently in the meditation hall. The rest of the day is full of hard work. Usually it is a time when speaking is not allowed. The monks are left in silence and there is nothing else to do except to practice Zen.

The rules for Sesshin are different from monastery to monastery. Sometimes it takes just a few days, but I have also heard of Sesshins which took a whole month.

As I already mentioned earlier, Sesshin is not considered vacation. It is hard work. Sitting in lotus form is painful after a couple of hours, but your feet are really going to kill you if you sit this way for days. You need to concentrate all the time, no matter how tired you are.

Monasteries are sometimes open to visitors. You might be able to join a Sesshin of your local Zen group. But you might also benefit from the idea of a Sesshin without taking a month off and living like a monk.

When I work hard, I find that my ego grows. Suddenly my work becomes more and more important and my

customers or boss can affect me on a personal level. I
consider myself important. And this is the time when I take
a "Sesshin".

Before I started to attend actual Sesshins, my "Sesshin"
was simply a holiday. One just needs to make sure it is a
real holiday. Step out of the world's business. Abstain from
the computer. Enjoy the real, non-virtual world. There is
family. There is nature. There are a lot of fantastic sports
activities waiting. Concentrate on making good food. Visit
friends. Care for your garden. There are many options
outside of our professional environment.

At the time of your Sesshin, body, health, and balance
are the most important. At office times, most of your work
is done with your mind. But at Sesshin time your body
should get more priority.

Defeat the Mind Monkey

"The mind is like a monkey" is a Buddhist saying[17]. The
mind cannot stand still. One idea follows the other. In
the office, the monkey has everything it needs to get us
distracted. Social networks and interesting blogs are just
one click away. The mind monkey alone is already hard to
defeat. But the monkey has a friend: the horse. The horse's
will whispers "I want to talk to my friend. *I want to!*" at
times you simply don't have a minute to spare. Both in

---

[17]I do not know about the origin, but this phrase along with the "horse's will"
is often referred to in Buddhist literature. Please also see this Wikipedia article
for more information: http://en.wikipedia.org/wiki/Mind_monkey

combination are enemies to concentrated work.

One thing which helps to stay focused is to clean your desk. We can also clean our computer, but it's not possible to clean it completely. Even when we disable a few URLs, we always find other interesting sites. We could uninstall our messenger software, but we might need it later.

In the past years I found a few strategies which helped me a lot to stay focused. I did not invent these and in many cases you can read a lot more about them on the internet.

To-Do Lists

When I create a note, it is most likely to get an idea out of my mind. I am no longer afraid of forgetting about it. I started with using simple but long lists for all my to-dos, but found out they are not readable. So I created several lists sorted by priority.

For the long term I have the A, B, and C lists. A means "top priority" and it needs to be done in the current week. The B list shows items which can wait for next week or even a bit later, until they become A priorities. The C list shows items which are not so important. Some items on this list are never done. This list is more or less a reminder of ideas. Sometimes they turn out well and then they make it to a B list.

Usually my A list is pretty full and keeps me busy for the whole week. If I am lucky I can perform all A-tasks in the same week. Sometimes it is not possible and it is a sign that I am either overcommitted or need a helping hand. If I am quick, I start working on B-tasks.

I plan my week every Monday, early in the morning. Years before I did my planning on Sunday evening, as it was recommended in a book I read. But I couldn't sleep very well when I recognized how much work awaited me. So I am up a little earlier on Monday now instead.

A weekly plan is still important for me. I believe it is not important how long you work; it is more important how many tasks you complete. I always set a high but realistic bar for myself. And I am highly motivated to reach this bar.

There is a drawback with to-do lists: if there are too many tasks on them they might frustrate you. I decided to allow myself to forget things. I do not plan unimportant tasks or tasks which are not business related. I accept that I am human. I am allowed to forget—no need to plan swimming, buying a book, or calling an old friend. These things will come to my mind when I want them. I just make sure I have enough time to let them happen.

There are a few great tools which offer a more advanced way to work with lists. If you like lists you should check out Workflowy[18] or Wunderlist[19].

I have meanwhile extended my to-do list system with Kanban (see later) and use to-do lists just for the tasks of the current day.

Emails: The Two-Minute-Rule and More

Mini-tasks like reading an email, responding to an event request, or making a call for a business partner's birthday

---

[18]http://www.workflowy.com
[19]http://www.wunderlist.com

draw away your attention quickly. If you are aware that you need to do it and you already wasted valuable seconds on it, perform the task when it takes less than two minutes. If the task takes longer than two minutes, write it on a to-do list. The only problem with this strategy is that it might happen that you get too many of these tasks. I had a time where I would get an email every three minutes. My email client would notify me of every incoming email. I would read it and 99% of the mails would be archived immediately. The rest of the mails were all important, but could wait for a couple of hours.

According to the two-minute-rule, I was right. I got distracted and was allowed to clean up my inbox. But the distraction was too much. I decided to reduce my overall email time and simply switched off the email client for most of the day.

I spent a while properly configuring my email filters. Many of the emails can be archived/deleted automatically. In Open-Source projects, where one can get tons of mail, it is crucial to filter or label the mail to your preference. Filters help you to read mail later without forgetting to.

If you reach a clean inbox then you did well.

I achieved a clean inbox with filtering and three special labels: "To-Read", "To-Print", and "Later". I would check these labels from time to time.

In addition I created a personal Wiki on one of my webservers. I store some knowledge there; it's a kind of virtual notebook. A couple of people prefer Evernote[20] which lets you more easily store knowledge. I prefer my Wiki and for web links I use Pocket[21].

The Pomodoro Technique

The Pomodoro Technique[22] is a method to keep focused on a single task. You can find plenty of information about it on the Pomodoro website[23]. If you find the following description interesting, you should look at it.

Basically it all starts with a to-do list. Create one and sort the to-dos based on priority. Then, take a kitchen timer and set it to twenty-five minutes. Work on the first task for that time and try hard to focus on it (that's called the Pomodoro). When the timer rings take a break for a few minutes. Then start with the next Pomodoro. Every four Pomodoros take a longer break, like twenty-five to thirty minutes.

The creator of this method recommends creating tasks which do not take longer than five to seven Pomodoros. He furthermore explains that you should track your unplanned events (phone calls, etc.) on your to-do list. If necessary, you should add a new to-do on your list, but try to work again on your Pomodoro as soon as possible.

The Pomodoro Technique is very motivating and leads

---

[20]http://evernote.net

[21]http://www.getpocket.com

[22]The Pomodoro Technique® and Pomodoro™ are registered trademarks of Francesco Cirillo.

[23]http://www.pomodorotechnique.com

to good results, if handled with care. I have seen somebody shout at his wife when she called him in the middle of a Pomodoro.

One needs some practice to get five to seven Pomodoros done. Don't be disappointed if you don't make it the first time. Pomodoro is exhausting if followed strictly. Don't forget to sleep when you are tired.

The Chain

Jerry Seinfeld is an actor. Brad Isaac[24] met him when he was a touring comedian and wrote an article on Lifehacker about it (Isaac, 2013).

Brad asked Jerry how one could become a better comic. Jerry responded, one must simply write better jokes and practice every day. If you have ever learned to play a musical instrument you know that "practice every day" is pretty hard and you need a lot of discipline for it.

Jerry developed a calendar system which helped him. Basically he printed a monthly calendar on a sheet of paper and when he practiced he made a big red cross on it. After a few days, the calendar was full of red crosses which he called "the chain". There is just one rule to follow: don't break the chain.

I used the chain system to write the first draft of this book. I managed to keep the chain, with a few exceptions. I felt regret when I did not have the time to write and the

---

[24]You can read more from Brad on his blog: http://www.persistenceunlimited.com/

next day I restarted the chain with the hope to not break it again.

This book contains several chapters. Between the chapters I took breaks. I had to think and reconsider the things I wrote. It was simply not possible for me to keep the chain for the whole book: sometimes I was simply out of creativity. Thus I broke the big book chain into multiple chapter chains, which worked much better for me.

"The Chain" is a technique I use very often, especially when learning about new technologies.

Kanban

Kanban is great when to-do lists alone are no longer enough. Originally made for the automotive industry, it has become a method for software development as well. There are differences between the original method and how programmers use it, but it doesn't matter. Kanban is flexible and you are encouraged to make it fit into your system.

It is easy: I take a big sheet of paper and divide it with a marker into four regions: "To-Do", "Progress", "Test", and "Done". It's called the Kanban line. In addition, I create another sheet of paper on a separate wall. I call it the "idea board". Then I make Post-its for each task and stick them on the idea board.

When I decide to work on an idea, I move the Post-it to the "To-Do" section. This is a kind of commitment. I am actually willing to do this, it's like having them on my A-grade to-do list.

When I start with a task, I move it to "Progress".

The progress region should only contain a few tasks. My personal maximum is four items. Depending on the volume of tasks you should consider a smaller number. More than four is, in most cases, not recommended.

Some tasks need to go to "Test". This may be when a customer needs to confirm my action or when I wait for some outcome from a third party (for example, when I send this book to the printer and wait for it to return).

Finally there is a "Done" section. You could throw away your finished Post-its, but I found it very motivating to keep them for a while. If it fills up quickly I am making good progress. If nothing changes after a while, my tasks are too big or I am too slow.

I use pen and paper and my wall is full of Post-its. It is very easy for me to oversee all the things I have in mind. But there are plenty of digital Kanban boards out there, some of them for free in a basic version.

Two boards which I like are:

- Kanbanery[25]
- AgileZen[26]

I tried both systems and like them both very much. Still I am more the pen-and-paper person. Actually I use only a paper calendar and not any smartphone calendars.

If you are interested in why I prefer paper, here we go:

---

[25]http://www.kanbanery.com
[26]http://www.agilezen.com

- Pricing: It is cheaper. You just need to pay for paper, Post-its and a pen. Except the huge dimensions of paper I use everything else was already on my desk.
- Learning: Writing by hand is a great learning tool. It forces you to slow down and focus on your thoughts or ideas. Writing engages your body and improves recall.(The Telegraph[27])
- Data safety: The cloud is not as safe as many of us think. Amazon has lost cloud data in 2011[28]. Hackers might attack the services you use and even corrupt backups. Some cloud services are simply not safe from failure. And your local hard drive might fail. You would need backups and if you store data on a network drive, you need to take care of read/write permissions. With paper, I don't need to deal with that. Only if my office burned down, would I have no backup. But in this case my Kanban board is the least of my problems.
- Easy setup: five minutes of fun paperwork and you are done.
- Offline support: with paper it is possible to turn off the computer, sit back and just think. Distraction simply does not happen.
- Customization: I am able to customize the workflow how I like it, without reading a manual. The idea

---

[27]http://www.telegraph.co.uk/education/educationnews/8271656/Write-it-dont-type-it-if-you-want-knowledge-to-stick.html

[28]You can find a lot of information about this meltdown in your favorite search engine. For a detailed post mortem analysis about the whole case, you should visit Amazon AWS directly: http://aws.amazon.com/de/message/65648/

board is basically not supported by the tools I mentioned earlier.

- Overview: All items with one look. No scrolling.
- Burn-Out Safe: My Kanban board stays in the office. I don't need to look at it from the living room, nor do I want to move things around in my free time.
- Fun!: I simply love this way and moving things around manually. It's inspiring.

But there are also benefits with digital versions.

- Distributed Teams: I love my colleagues, but they should not always look into my office (I work from home and have a small kid, maybe you understand).
- Workflows Which Inspire: Digital Kanban boards sometimes allow you to play with the suggested workflow, which might inspire you to change the way you work. They have some experience with this, while with a manual Kanban you are left with your own creativity.
- Changes: Digital versions let you change your board more quickly. Dragging and dropping five items at once is simply faster.
- Paper is nice, but you cannot do Control-Z.

I am attracted by the "offline" feature of manual Kanban. But when I am working in a team I move on to something digital which can be shared.

Don't Become an Extremist

I am a working machine. I have a lot of hours each week. I sometimes write emails at unusual times, like Saturday nights. But when I get a response from a full-time employee of a company in the same night, I am a bit worried about my colleague. There is a difference between geeky freelancers and reliable employees.

As a freelancer I can arrange my worktime as I need to. Sometimes I can simply turn on the computer and just work twenty hours.

As a full-time employee I don't have such a freedom. I need to make my forty hours, no matter what. Sure I have holidays and such; but the constant number of forty hours + overtime is always haunting me. In many cases you can't go to a break room and take a nap. When you get a phone call that your kid is sick, you cannot simply drive home: often people work far away from where our actual life happens. The old model of 9-to-5 or forty hours did work much better when there was no mobile technology. When you went home, you were gone. But now you have forty hours, some overtime, AND you are always connected to work with the shiny tablet you recently got from your boss.

On the one hand, there are fixed "core business times". On the other hand, there is "always-online". This combination asks for trouble.

A good bunch of people I have worked with are now very proud of the tons of email they have managed to work through, with the specs they rewrote, and the great service they provided, when they discussed a new feature with the customer – early in the morning on Sunday. The new metric for a successful day seems to be the level of exhaustion.

Imagine: Monday morning, the door is opening. Your colleague comes in and says: "I had such a great weekend. I slept all of Saturday, had a long breakfast on Sunday, and went out swimming on Sunday." No Blackberry? Haven't learned any new great technology? What a lazy guy! But if he comes in with red eyes, tired, and says: "Hectic weekend. I made an emergency call with a customer. Have you had the time to look into feature B? I promised him that I would..." Heroic! This mate sacrificed his weekend for the company and finally for your job. Shouldn't you look into feature B this evening at home?

Why is the level of exhaustion so important to us?

Our software projects are huge these days—is it related to that? When you craft something with your own hands, you can see the result and can be proud of it. You can show it to others.

On the other hand, clean up your code for a week. It doesn't add new features, nobody comes to your desk and congratulates you for such a brilliant clean-up. Instead, several weeks' worth of work sometimes is described as "just one button which sends a report". Building a product is the work of many people. Sometimes you just write code on a specific part nobody will ever see. The whole product is nothing you alone made. So many people, so little the chance that you can be proud of it. You need to measure your involvement differently, like: I made a hundred commits, wrote a hundred emails and had ten meetings for this software version.

In an ideal world, our software architecture includes well-composed artifacts which are then handcrafted by small teams who can be proud of what they do. Even better, if the composed artifacts become visible to others. You are suffering from fragmentation if you have twenty developers and just one component to build: nobody can identify with this whole mess of a code, people have fragmented responsibility.

With overcommitted people and the way we measure our success in mind, Scrum becomes a turbo boost. And a risk.

The agile world has got a hammer which makes every problem a nail: Scrum. Scrum is a perfect optimization of your workflow in many cases, seen from the project management's point of view. From the developer's point of view it is also good: you get things done. But Scrum has its risks when the team does not pay attention to the human factor. As humans we simply cannot put forty hours workload in a forty hour week. We need time to reflect on our work. We need to perform minor refactorings. We need to read through code which we have already looked at. Sometimes we need to think! And we cannot estimate the time we need to think. We don't know how much we need to think; do we need to rethink the whole model? Do we have our full-thinking-competence today or are we tired, because we slept badly? We need to accept we are humans. We cannot break ourselves down into numbers.

Scrum lets you look at your tasks with a clock in the background. It is tempting to just work through everything until you are done. But, hey, it is software development. Things change while we look at them, like the Heisenberg thing. And be it only if we are to tired to work efficient on Tuesday. Things like that happen. Deal with it when you do Scrum planning: don't forget the humans behind the Scrum-roles. If you understand that, your estimations are way better.

I wonder how Van Gogh's pictures would have looked like if he had applied Scrum to his work. Guess we wouldn't know his name today. Creativity under pressure—I simply don't believe it works (exceptions are confirming this rule). From my own experience as a hobby musician: I cannot compose anything when I am loaded with work. I need time to dream, to relax, and think unusual thoughts.

Software is crafted with the mind. It is a creative work, even when we apply other creative works like ready-to-use design patterns. Sometimes we work on no-brainers, that's true. But as we all know, we software people should constantly look at the code in the neighborhood and identify bug patterns or other things which would make our software more reliable and understandable. The art of software often is the art of minimizing your code. You can't do that when you are constantly under time pressure and delivering an endless stream of features.

The solution is simple: if you can't stop focusing on work tasks, look at your family, free time, etc., as a task. Plan it, do it, enjoy it as well as you can. Calculate the human factor into your Scrum sprints. Don't measure your success on your overtime and switch off your mobile on the weekend. You'll always be more productive on Monday.

If you work on a system which is too huge to be proud of, change it. Software systems should not only be maintainable, extensible, and reliable—they must also be enjoyable! A good system is one we love to work with—if we are proud that we could contribute a little to it, it can't be so wrong. The best gardeners are those who enjoy taking a walk through the garden.

I wrote a lot about how I changed my thinking and how I dealt with stress. I also wrote about tools which helped me to keep my mind clean. But in the end, these are just tools, not a religion. You need to carefully use and choose your tools. Do what works good for you and when it doesn't give you anything back, walk away and try something else. Unfortunately, it does not often happen that projects throw away their methods. If they started with Scrum, they stick with it. No matter what. Even when there are times when Scrum simply doesn't fit.

Make sure you don't become an extremist of any kind. It is the middle way which counts.

Zen Is About You

No matter from which direction the wind blows: stand safely on your feet. Your life is about you alone.

Life is not only happiness and joy. Life always has its good and bad times. You even have bad times if you are rich and own the latest gadgets. In the same vein, our lives are not "worse" just because of overtime or less money.

Others Don't Treat Me Well

Today's TV and other media channels want to make us believe that we need to to be 100% happy to live a good life. They claim happiness is achieved by being rich, beautiful, and healthy. They have a couple of products waiting for us to reach this "happiness".

Nonsense. Happiness comes, Happiness goes. It's just normal.

It doesn't matter if you are on the beach or at work; you are allowed to be happy. And you don't need any product from any company to be happy.

We are responsible for our own fortune. It might be your boss's fault that you have overtime, but it is your fault to be so unhappy about it. It is, of course, fine if you defend yourself from having too much overtime. As a human you can walk many directions and you can make your own decisions. Take the consequences or leave them. After all, good times will follow bad times, and bad times will follow good times.

I mentioned earlier that software developers should stay at least for two years or a little longer with a company. As long as you can argue it, you might break this rule. In fact, you should break any rules you have heard so far if they are not good for you.

If you are not ready for breaking the rules you might find some comfort with talking to others. As a developer you might have access to local usergroups. These are groups of people who share interest in a technology, like a programming language. Speaking with others you trust might help not only with making you feel better, maybe it even helps you to find a new job.

> All problems come from mind.
>
> —Bodhidharma (Red Pine, 1987)

One day at work, a colleague entered the room. He mumbled "good morning" and sat down in his chair. Seconds later, he heavily typed on his keyboard. Around him was a cold atmosphere, full of anger. It turned out he did not get a salary raise. Another developer he knew worked for a different company and earned 100€ more. Not that he really needed the money—it was a matter of principle. He thought he was just the better developer and deserved the 100€. He did not need the money anyways. After taxes, he couldn't even fuel his car. The cold atmosphere held on for a couple of days and he constantly complained how unfair he was treated. He totally ignored the fact that he had already earned a lot of money and had gotten a salary raise recently. His problem was actually coming from his own mind. Others would have loved to have his job. Still he was unhappy and even spread these emotions among his colleagues.

Where I live, when something bad happens at least one person says it is "bad luck" or "fate". All problems seem to come from outside.

Somebody is a drinker? He might have had a traumatic experience. Somebody is poor? It might be the government's fault. If someone suddenly earns millions of dollars, he might either be reckless or he manipulates people. When we don't know what to say because somebody died, it is all God's will.

Nobody knows what is behind the scenes. Maybe it is God's will. But even so, He gives us the freedom to think and act on our own. Does He want us to be jealous of 100€? I doubt it.

Maybe it is not fate, God, or our bad childhood which makes our lives worse. It is the way we think about it. Fate makes our life a burden, because we believe it so.

I Deserve It

Many people consider their mind and their thoughts to be the most important aspects of their being, but Bodhidharma thought different. In his teachings, thoughts are byproducts of the mind. Like stomach acid is a by-product of the stomach.

While there are important thoughts, there are more often unimportant thoughts mixed in. For example, when you wander through a desert it is important to know the way, but not to think about the taste of a cold drink.

My mind constantly tells me what I want. It whispers about tablet pcs until I buy one. Then the mind says: "Well done! You really deserved it! Now I am happy." Really? Everything is in movement and there is no constant in life. Happiness will go away. My mind will sooner or later come up with new wishes.

I know there are other people who think they deserve the latest tablets or phones. Recently I saw photos of people standing for hours outside of a shop, waiting for a new smartphone. Guess their mind is confident when whispering "you deserve it". Is the mind right? I don't know. But I believe everybody deserves food and clean water.

In Ghana, Africa, people would be glad to have food and clean water. This is the place where your old smartphone will most likely go, according to the movie E-

Wasteland.[29] Jeremy Hance documented how 200,000 tons of e-waste arrives at this place annually. Boys and young men come out of the slums and "recycle" it, barehanded. Small fires burn down your waste, carrying toxic smoke everywhere. With the little money they make, they can buy food and clean water.

The things we "deserve" so much are ending up in places like Ghana. Manufacturers chose the cheapest way to get rid of the waste to maximize profit. The "recycling process" is toxic because it costs money to make it healthier.

I took this quote with me from the movie:

> It is essential that we understand and appreciate that we make decisions every day that directly or indirectly affect others elsewhere on the planet.
>
> —David Fedele

My mind fools me often with what I deserve or do not. I try to not put so much weight on all the thoughts I have from time to time. What I deserve and what my mind says is good for me, is just crap for others who are struggling to get daily bread.

---

[29]The trailer and order details can be found here: http://www.e-wastelandfilm.com/

I Had a Bad Childhood

In 1880, a boy was born in Japan. At the age of four his mother died. At seven, his father died and he lived with his uncle from then on. A little time later, his uncle died too and he was raised by a gambler and a prostitute. The gambler often asked the young boy to look out for the police when he needed some quick money.

Obviously the boy had a bad childhood. He could have become a gambler or some sort of criminal. At the very least he should have become a drinker. Instead he took three kilos of rice and a few coins with which he bought beans. He traveled four days and nights and finally reached the Eiheiji temple to become a Zen monk. For days he just ate raw rice. The monks would not let him in, so he stood for two more days and nights before the temple, without food or water. Finally the monks allowed him to enter and work there as an errand boy.

He was at the bottom of the hierarchy. Even the cleaning lady did not treat him with respect. One day the boy decided to practice Zazen in a quiet and mostly unused room. He sat down and meditated as he has observed from the monks. Suddenly, the door opened and the cleaning lady came in. She stared at him for a second. Then she bowed and silently left the boy alone.

It did not take long before the boy became a monk and got a new name: Kôdô Sawaki.

Kôdô Sawaki then became one of the most important

Zen masters of the past century.[30] He knew that Zazen was one of the noblest things humans can do. He continued with his practice until he died.

Guess a good number of people would have ended up as gamblers themselves.

This story shows, that—in theory—poverty is no reason to abstain from right livelihood. It is also good proof that one can have a bad childhood and still have a good life. I didn't have the chance to go to university when I was young. But with hard work, a lot of overtime and a bit luck, it was possible for me to to become a professional programmer.

I Know It Better

Ajahn Brahm is a Buddhist monk who wrote a fantastic book. It's called "Opening the Door of Your Heart" and contains a lot of modern stories which make you think. He is not a Zen monk but follows a Thai lineage, though this does not make his writing any less valuable.

While meditating deep in the forests of Thailand, he had to eat food most of us programmers would not have touched. The meals consisted of a sticky ball of rice, crowned by a cooked frog, containing all its innards. For some reason the innards were considered very tasty. When the monks ran out of frog, fish curry was served, which was so old that

---

[30]Kôdô Sawaki's life has been described by Koshiya Shusoku. I am not sure if it has been translated into English. The German translation appeared in the book "Zen ist die größte Lüge aller Zeiten" (Sawaki, 2005).

it included maggots.

Ajahn didn't complain and kept on meditating. And one day he woke up and felt ... enlightened. He wanted to tell his abbot after the dinner. He really felt lucky as he saw not only the old fish curry was served this day but also a fresh pork curry. The abbot took the first from this delicious fresh food, and he took a lot. When he was done he took the pork curry and mixed it into the fish curry. While working with his wooden spoon he said: "It's basically all the same."[31]

Ajahn became angry, really angry, because he simply wanted that fresh-made pork curry. At this point he suddenly realized that he wasn't enlightened at all. As he wrote, real enlightenment does not let you to curse your abbot. The enlightened do not have a favorite food.

This story showed me I can be wrong, even when I believe I am absolutely right. The mind sometimes fools us.

It's Your Life

You cannot have a good life because there are too many problems?

---

[31]The original language was Thai, which Brahm translated into English, which was then translated to German, which has been translated back to English by me. The original is surely a bit different.

> Whatever happens to you is your life.
>
> —Kôdô Sawaki (Sawaki, 2008)

If you lost body parts, you would really have some trouble. But it would still be your life. You could not change it. You have been fired because you are not efficient enough? Maybe you aren't good at what you do. Maybe you are. You'll never know. Just do it as well as you can and try to work on your skills. Then you know there is nothing to worry about.

> Every day is a good day.
>
> —Kôdô Sawaki (Sawaki, 2008)

Your manager was angry? Your wife screamed at you because you came home late after a horrible working day? You cannot change it. It is a day of your life. With a limited number of days, you cannot do anything about it.

If you cannot change it, accept it. Maybe you have reasons. Reflect on them. Prepare to do it better next time, if possible. After all, you need to accept it.

No Ego

What Is Ego?

I did not realize that ego might be a problem until I studied Buddhism. I thought about it for a long time. What does it mean? Why is it so bad? I am still thinking about it. While I was at first a sceptic when I was told to get rid of my ego, I later thought differently. In Zen it is often said, one must forget himself. Just existing in the now without an ego. Ego makes you attached to things.

In many parts of the world we celebrate the individual. We often think that only our desires and wishes make us special. Some spike their hair up 50cm high. Others shoot needles through their eyebrows. Some believe in a career which gives them status and titles. Some define themselves with their programming skills.

What happens if you take away their skills, careers, or body art? A car accident maybe or a sickness. When such an event happens, people act as if their life was ruined. Life becomes useless when the center of self definition is taken.

We need to see that we are not our wishes and desires. It is for sure a natural act that we grow up, develop tastes, and develop a way of life. For some reason we need to find an identity and want to be unique. But we need to learn that we are more than just what we do or want to do.

Friendships are often built on common interests and so

they might break. Friendships are also often defined with taking and giving; if you don't have the will to give, the friendship will die.

> Some live as there is no tomorrow; and when they are going to die, they behave as they would not have lived.
>
> —Kôdô Sawaki (Sawaki, 2005)

A single special event in life might cause someone to lose health, self definition, and friends. The ego is a dangerous thing.

Ego Makes You Do Things

We are attached to the I.

When I was young, I wanted to become a great programmer. In my imagination others would respect me for my skills. I wanted it so much that I decided to join a famous open-source group. That was not easy, because you can join only when you are invited by the group.

And you only get an invitation if you have shown that you are really committed to a project and its team. This strategy keeps the group healthy, as only people with a real interest can join and the other group members can intervene if they have any concerns.

For me, it was a great chance to show my programming skills to the world. I started writing patches and sent it to them. I did that for a while, but I wasn't invited. Instead, I learned there are other programmers who are way better than me. They looked at my patches and told me how to do it better. It was frustrating. Instead of showing my great skills, I was showing my incompetence. At work, everybody thought I had some great skills. But this was different. Instead of being a rockstar, I suddenly became a student.

I continued to code. It would look good on my CV. But I did not get an invite. At some point I started to think it would never happen. I gave up my plans to join the group. The code became a hobby and I changed my mind about it. I realized how much I learned and started to enjoy learning from the other, obviously better programmers. And when my work was almost ready for a first release, I found an invitation in my inbox. I accepted. But for a long time I forgot to add the group's name to my CV. It was no longer important.

It is said a man once came to Buddha. He said: "I want happiness." Buddha replied: "First remove the I. It is ego. Next remove the want. It is desire. Now see what is left."

This is what happened to me.

Today I try to do things because they feel right. I try to avoid doing things because my ego commands it.

Without regular meditation practice my ego starts to grow again. I can only recommend meditation practice if you want to work on your ego. Even if you believe you do not have an ego, you should meditate too; because in this case you are already under full control of your ego.

In general, comparing yourself to others will not lead to anything useful.

Egoless Programming

Jerry Weinberg once wrote about egoless programming (Weinberg, 1972).

He wrote we should put aside our ego at work and start reviewing our code. Show others our mistakes. Explain what we did wrong. And do the same for our colleagues. All that should happen in a friendly atmosphere. He said we are not our code and thus there is no room for personal feelings.

This is a nice idea. Unfortunately we have an ego and it is hard work to let it go. If we do not like the reviewer, it is easier to find something negative about him instead of accepting the results of the code review.

One could say the mind produces code and the ego makes you attached to it. There is a connection between what your mind produces and you. In a way, you are your code. What Weinberg proposes is to cut your mind from code. This can only be achieved by removing the ego.

As already mentioned this is a long road.

The Invisible Ego

In my career I have met a lot of people. I have never met an egoless person. Some people try to hide their ego, some display their ego very openly. For years I categorized the manifestation of egos in two different ways.

The first group have an active and aggressive ego. Code reviews are difficult. It is easy to make them upset and to make them look for negative things about yourself. Active egos might call you a nitpicker when you find a typo. They complain about the tight budget when you spot an architectural problem. They defend themselves even when there is nothing to defend.

The second group has a passive and more defensive ego. Code reviews might cause disappointment and frustration. Instead of taking the chance to improve skills, they are frustrated that they don't have the skills already—or they simply do not care. It is easy to make a passive ego feel stupid. Their ego has a low self esteem.

I started to observe people and thought I would learn from their egos. As a team leader, I had an excellent position for this. I explained a lot of technical things and reviewed a lot of code. So the more I learned about the others egos, the more I felt my ego was under control. For me, the others were either "active" or "passive".

But then I realized my mistake: I had forgotten my own ego. It was not under control, it was just hidden. I was experienced and everybody accepted that. I had the final word in discussions, everybody knew that. There was nothing which would provoke my ego so much as to make it visible.

I was aware that I enjoyed the situation of being the cool, experienced guy on the team. In fact, I may have had the biggest ego of them all. When I looked back, I realized my efforts to learn from others failed. I only looked at the failures of others, which made me blind to the big picture and to my own failures.

Back then, I learned that ego is often invisible to its owner. Believing you have no ego is probably a signal that you have a huge ego.

These days I know my ego will follow me and I have to fight it every second. I try to keep my awareness. When my mind tells me that I am going to lose control over my ego, I simply go to practice more meditation before it gets worse.

Shut Up

Gaken. This term describes your own opinion and the belief that you are an intelligent person. This is the reason for a lot of quarrels.

In a meeting there are many important people. Actually most people who attend a meeting believe they are in some way important. You aren't invited if you aren't important, right?

What happens if you are invited to a boring meeting with boring people? It's a perfect reason to complain about the waste of time but still think we are important because others cannot do without us.

Finally, even the people who are never asked to attend a meeting might think they are important; they have probably just been forgotten or simply undervalued.

An employee who really believes he is not important might either ruin the atmosphere or leave the company or both.

Important people often feel the obligation to contribute to each and every discussion whether helpful or not. It is easy to lose ourselves in senseless chatter and enjoy hearing ourselves talk. Poor colleagues are those who need to wait for a long time just to make sure everybody knows how important they are.

Innovation and creativity sometimes come from random thoughts. We need to differ between nonsense and important contributions. It is difficult. Before saying anything, I try to take a deep breath. This often helps me to see if I want to provoke somebody or just defend my standpoint because I cannot accept that I was wrong.

We need to hold a mirror before our minds to differentiate ego, knowledge, and experience. Strong negative feelings are often a sign of ego talk. Being tired or trying to impress your conversation partner are others.

Often it is enough to show support for an idea. We do not need to get into details if the purpose of the meeting is to look at the big picture. Sometimes it is hard to support a colleague's idea if we do not like them much. But we should. Others' success does not make you look bad. Let people with good ideas enjoy their fame. As a team leader, you do not need to be always the most creative, hardest working man with the best ideas. There is actually no competition.

I try to take ideas as ideas. If they need work, I try to work on them. If I need to understand more, I ask. If I do not like the idea I say it clearly and hopefully with a clear argument. But if the idea is good and I have nothing specific to add, I simply shut up.

Others may disagree and think there needs to be competition among co-workers. It should not be like that. A competition is only good if it is beneficial for all and, in some way, fun. But competitions for "careers" are senseless. Companies I know push the career competition. What they often get are not the most competent, but the most aggressive people. Maybe this works out, but it is not the way I want to live.

The people who believe their career is the most important in their lifes might annoy you. They will waste your time with nonsense and trivialities. There is most often nothing you can do about it. Before you get out of balance, you might want to try your mental ignore button or confront the person with what troubles you. Clear and honest words can help in many cases, but not all.

I am trying to live in a way that I avoid getting on anybody's nerves—including my own. I hope everybody would live like that.

If you wander through a forest and show beautiful flowers to a fellow who has just his goal in mind, he is most likely not impressed. His mind is filled with only his goal.

If you show the flowers to a fellow who wants to enjoy the beauty of this world, he will love it. In addition, he will reach his goal too.

Zen Is Hard Work

The term "Samadhi" means deep concentration. I have heard "Samadhi" also being used by Zen monks to refer to "hard work" in general. This includes work in the garden, repairing the monastery, and anything else that is necessary. If you have imagined monks sitting in their chairs while the ordinary people do the work, you are wrong. Monks are really hardworking folks, at least in the Zen monasteries I have heard of.

In some monasteries they wake up at 3am. They meditate, have breakfast, meditate, have lunch, relax, meditate, eat their evening meal and go to bed at 9:30pm. This is at Sesshin, one week or more of intense meditation. If you have ever tried to sit down for only one hour, you can imagine what hard work it is to meditate for so long.

Zen is hard work.

The Right Time for Zen Is Any Time

Zen is not spirituality. Zen is practiced with your body.

—Kôdô Sawaki (Sawaki, 2007)

Kôdô Sawaki explained your mind is expressed in your body and even more in your attitude towards life. With that he means Zen is not something which you do alone in your room. It is not something which is done with your mind only. Instead, you should practice Zen in every second of your life. Zen is your daily life. It also means we practice Zen when we go to the toilet, code software, and cook our meals. All of these and much more are Zen practice.

Practice Zen at any time even at work. It will change the way you think about your work.

Kôdô Sawaki said: "A day without work is a day without food." Work is important. But work is more than just bringing your daily bread to the table. It helps you stand safely with both feet on the ground. The news is full of rich people abusing drugs and alcohol. Without work it is easier to focus on the "I". Too much of everything nourishes your desires. When you are used to somebody else cleaning your toilet, you probably forget what a dirty task it is. Cleaning up your own mess and caring for your own household helps you to see yourself as what you are: human.

Career

When I started with Zen I had the dream of becoming a partner in the consulting company I worked for. I worked pretty hard and my body quickly drained of energy. I did not feel good. I started with Zen to avoid seeing my head explode. After a while I asked myself why I was about to sacrifice the next ten years or more to become a partner in that company. Suddenly I was not sure about it. Many people there were superficial. The projects were huge, but upon closer inspection, pretty boring.

Everyone wore ties and smiled all day. What would they do for their next promotion? I realized that though I needed work to earn a living, nobody was forcing me to live ten years among career oriented people. I realized that, for me, there is more to life: family, music, horseback riding. I would have to put my whole life on hold for a long time if I wanted to become a partner of the company. Maybe I would even die within that time. In ten years, I could start living again. But what prevents me from living now, the next ten years, and maybe even the rest of my life? Nothing.

I quit and joined another company. After a couple of years I quit there too, because the company changed its atmosphere and more or less asked the same from me: to pause my life and start a career, however it looked. Now I am working harder than ever before on my own company. I do not have a career goal anymore. My life is better. Surprisingly, I also have had more success in business.

A career does not mean you need to jump when a manager tells you. It seems people believe this will bring increase your paycheck. Well, maybe it does. But after all that you learn nothing except how to jump when somebody tells you. You are getting the job because of that. I really don't want a job just because I could follow a command. I am tired of working in companies which require that.

Instead, I want to work in companies which promote talent and passion. Who help me to develop, because they know I will develop the company. I want to work for companies which consist of humans, not managers.

In Germany, social workers and geriatric nurses are badly paid. Less people want to spend money on the old, weak, or sick. Nurses work hard, but if you speak with them, they seem to be incredibly happy with their job. They may be underpaid, but I never found a nurse who wanted to have my programming job. It leads me to the conclusion that a lower-paid job you can do with passion is better then a well-paid one which is boring. This doesn't mean these people don't deserve more just because they love their job. They definitely do, and we all will learn that when we need help ourselves in fifty years.

If you always code with your goal in mind, you might lose your way. And the way itself can be beautiful. There is much greatness in being a software developer. It is good whether you are a beginner or an expert. You need to live now and fill the role you are in, otherwise you will miss the fantastic experience of building a system.

The most impressive people I have met have made a career without spending too much energy on thinking about the career itself. They go to work and do what they need to do with passion and with all energy they have. These people are natural leaders. They do not have power "over" people, but power "with" people (Forsyth, 2009). Others will recognize them and follow. Do not look at goals like becoming a manager one day. If you are good and a leader by nature, you will get the role from that alone. Do not believe people who are trying to tell you that you need to pause your life to earn glory later. They just want to control you.

The Peter Principle brings up an important point. Wikipedia defines it as: "a belief that, in an organization where promotion is based on achievement, success, and merit, that organization's members will eventually be promoted beyond their level of ability. The principle is commonly phrased, 'employees tend to rise to their level of incompetence.' "

In short, you are promoted until you have reached a level were you fail the most. This is basically where career ladders lead. For that reason you should think twice about where your path should lead. There is always an option to say "no" to a promotion and just do what you like to do and what you are good at.

You Cannot Separate Your Mind from Your Body

A friend of mine is a computer admin. He reads a lot. He did not manage to get a degree from university, but when you talk with him you can see he is pretty intelligent and able to adapt and connect different philosophical patterns quickly. It sounds appealing to be a thinker like he is; but it isn't. He suffers from depression. I don't know the root cause of his depression. My best guess is that he understands so much of philosophy that everything sounds wrong, boring, or senseless. He does not see much sense in life and he does not have his own way. You cannot help him with rationality. He needs to find a way out himself.

He lives a life of thoughts.

In summer, we had a long discussion on philosophical topics. At some point he said he would be glad if he could simply separate mind from body. Without a body, he might be able to think without any restrictions.

Is it the weird idea of a dreamer or the wish of a postmodern human? With biohackers[32] among us, it does not sound so much like Frankenstein anymore.

The whole idea sounds bizarre and surreal. But look at our lives as computer programmers: we sit mostly without moving in unhealthy positions in front of a monitor and stare into it for hours. We work with our minds. When we have a model to a complex problem, we visualize our thoughts with minimal effort through the keyboard. Ten hours a day. At lunch time we move our bodies to a nearby restaurant and eat. At home we relax in front of a TV. The question is whether we haven't already separated our bodies from our minds. Have we not lost the connection to the real world and true life?

After I started with Zen, I also decided to spend my spare time in the real world. I chose to play Shakuhachi, a Japanese bamboo flute which also can be used for meditation purposes.

I was inspired by Watazumi, a Zen priest and famous

---

[32]Biohackers are people who implant technical modifications in their body to extend their abilities.

Shakuhachi player (Watazumi, 2012[33]). He developed his way for fifty years and emphasized the connection between body and mind. He said breathing and physical strength are tied to a healthy mind. His day started at 3:30am. He practiced with the Jō wand—a 4.2 foot long wooden staff used in martial arts. This practice was followed by six hours of Shakuhachi playing. It is known he did that for at least 3000 consecutive days.

> And when you consider rhythm, rhythm is not just simply rhythm; rhythm is the movement of the entire body down to its last cell.
>
> —Watazumi Roshi (Watazumi, 2012)

When I feel that I am caught in the virtual world, I play Shakuhachi for longer than usual. I do sports. I have Watazumi in mind, who practiced until he died.

My friend reminded me of Nietzsche.

When you are in that virtual mode for too long, your reality becomes a virtual one. If you solve complex technical problems for too long, you will finally become a complex technical problem yourself.

The original quote was more drastic:

---

[33][#watazumi]

Whoever fights monsters should see to it that in the
process he does not become a monster. And when
you look into the abyss, the abyss also looks into you.

—Friedrich Nietzsche (Nietzsche, 1886)

When we become older, we will suffer from the lack of
attention we gave to our bodies. We will ask ourselves, why
we suffer from sickness. The answer is simple—we became
monsters. We became virtual people.

As long as we have muscles, a beating heart, a pulse,
and cells, we should think differently.

Learn

The only constant in life is the fact that there is no constant.
Life is always moving on, like a flowing river. The skills
which are in demand are changing. Programmers need to
refine their skills every day, but they are also forced to
learn to quickly change the way they think or to learn a
completely new skill set. We constantly learn about new
businesses. We face new technology daily. What we code
is always different. There is nothing ever the same, even
when we implement the same or similar requirements. If
you reuse code the integration is different.

Last year I started a project with plain jQuery. Today
I would never start a project without AngularJS. It is even

hard to recommend anything to a customer who demands sustainability.

For Confucius, a wise man who influenced Eastern ethics a lot, learning was crucial.

> The best men are born wise. Next come those who grow wise by learning: then, learned, narrow minds. Narrow minds, without learning, are the lowest of the people.
>
> —Confucius (Eliot, 2001)

The Forester

A good forester knows that every tree is different. He knows roots grow differently. He is aware of every tree, of the sun, the earth and all the animals. He will consider all of that before he cuts a tree. Bad foresters walk quickly through the wood and cut down trees to make as much profit as possible in the shortest time possible.

We need to learn about our environment too. It is easy to learn a new programming language, but it is not so easy to connect loose ends of your knowledge to each other. When we learn, we need to take time to make and to find those connections. Otherwise we will be able to scratch only the surface of our work.

Theory Needs to Become Practice

"The lowest of us are those who do not learn," said Confucius. But learning does not mean only to sit at home and read books. You must practice what you learn or it is only theory. It does not make any sense to learn about a programming language and never use it. You haven't learned it until you made a project with it.

This example seems very obvious. But still there are a lot of people I know who do this senseless learning. They buy books—on communication skills, on methodology, on "how to live a better life"—and then they do nothing with the new knowledge. They read it to soothe their conscience, I often say. I am a bit closer to some and can ask them why they do not simply practice what they have learned. "It isn't so easy," is often the answer. Sure, but if changing were so easy, we wouldn't need books for advice.

Do you want to improve your people skills? Just be a nice person. If you aren't a nice person it will become difficult for you. Unfortunately no book will help you out with this. It is only you who can do this change.

If you don't really want to practice the theory, you can save the time and do something else.

Learn from Others

It is easy to learn from others, and only your own ego will prevent you from doing so.

Others might have a more extensive knowledge, even when they are young. If you can't learn from their code, learn from their behavior, their fears, or their likes and dislikes. If they dislike you, learn why. If they like you, learn why. If you write good code, and somebody complains about it: Why? Why does your colleague want to replace your code with a worse solution?

One thing which helped me to learn learning from others was when I started with Open Source. The core value of the Apache Software Foundation is: Community over Code. I met many great people during that time. Not only on the mailing lists, but also in person at conferences. They were all nice people and now, when I have a problem, I can reach out to them and they can usually help me.

I am not too shy to ask questions when I do not understand. Even when I am expected to know something, I ask sometimes simple questions. I don't care so much if it sounds dumb. Nobody knows everything. In Open Source communities your questions are visible to the public. Some are afraid of that. Potential employers might look at what you have asked. But what is the problem? If you ask nicely, you have nothing to fear. Learning is nothing you need to be ashamed of.

My first code contributions were horrible. I sent them well intentioned, but they were always rejected for a tons of reasons. It went on for quite a while like this. It was frustrating at first, but it was also a great chance. Sometimes people who were known for their extraordinary work on a specific domain were reviewing my code and giving me feedback. Open Source work has taught me more than any training.

If you want to really learn, join an Open Source community and start hacking with others. It's rewarding.

Don't Become a Job Title Addict

Are you a senior programmer? What makes you a "senior"? Is it your age? Is it the time you have been on a project? Or is it your incredible and hard-to-beat knowledge of a technology? I admit, when I was young and a so-called junior programmer I always wanted to become a senior programmer. Probably just because others were listening to the seniors on my team and I liked the respect they got.

Becoming a senior programmer is not so easy actually. You could work for ten years and be the only living expert in a certain programming language and others might call you a Geek, but not an Expert. You could learn thousands of different technologies but people might call you a guy who is a junior in every technology. And if you become a guy who always knows everything and explains it to others all the time, you just get called an idiot.

Today we face a true buzzword insanity. People hunt for job titles as if they might make them better people. If some people would put the same effort into treating colleagues nice as they hunt for job titles, the world would be great.

There are Software Architects, Agile Managers, Software Developers, Consultants, Analyst Consultants, Senior Analyst Programmers, and so on.

The term "programmer" is used as a synonym for

people who are good with syntax but have no clue otherwise. It's bad to be a programmer these days. In 2011, Patrick McKenzie wrote a blog post with the name "Don't Call Yourself A Programmer, And Other Career Advice" (Kenzie, 2011). As he wrote, calling yourself a Programmer might sooner or later lead to losing your job. You must call yourself a "value creator" or something similar.

Basically, others try this with cryptic job titles like Senior Consultant Architect. If there is some space left on the business card, you could put Agile, SEO, REST or some other trendy term. We practice job title marketing.

I don't get how people differentiate the terms "programmer" and "developer". I have heard people say programmers are some folks from India, but the real developers are those who plan a system and pay the Indian programmers to do the typing.

> A programmer, computer programmer, developer, or coder is a person who writes computer software.
>
> —Wikipedia

No difference for Wikipedia. I also can't see a big difference between rich industrial-nation programmers/developers and colleagues from classic outsourcing countries.

Searching for a difference based on location or task is the wrong way to go. It easily leads to prejudice. It's arrogant.

And it divides the world in thirds. The first world is the ones with the real developers, architects, and project managers. The successful, the beautiful. The world with the great ideas and great dreams. The second world is the one with the people we just call programmers who do the coding work for little money. And the third world is that one to which we send our electronic waste, because they can't even code.

There are great developers living in each corner of the world. You cannot say a programmer who implements a specification is worse than the guy who wrote the specification. You simply don't know.

A job title should describe what you do most at your time. They just give outsiders an idea if you are the right person to speak to. A title doesn't make you more or less valuable. You simply cannot distinguish from a job title if somebody is good with his job or not.

Eventually software people become programmers in a way. It doesn't matter whether you are planning software or a tester, or checking on requirements with customers. All are part of the software programming process, which makes them programmers.

In my own company, I am CEO, software architect, tester, administrator, and hacker. I am a programmer. If I am hiring a guy to code for me, I am still a programmer.

Choosing a good job title can be an art form. Express what you are doing in one or two words. It's almost impossible with the wide range of tasks we need to perform each day. A good job title is expressive and minimal.

Running Water

No one can see their reflection in running water. It is only in still water that we can see.

—Taoist Proverb

At work, we run like hamsters in their wheels. Phone calls, Twitter, emails, some code which needs to work despite the horrible problems which should not be there. And our customers really don't care about these problems, they just want to make the deadline.

We are more than just programmers. We need to breathe and we need time to reflect on ourselves. We need to celebrate our victories and we need to feel our bones, skin, and muscles. We need to clear our mind of the problems of other people from time to time and maintain our own life.

In short: we need time for our own thoughts and emotions, for better or worse. We need to calm the running water of our lives.

To calm down, you need to do something other than work. Some think hobbies are just "fun" or "distracting". For them only working time is real life. But they are wrong. If you can afford to have a hobby you should maintain it. It helps express yourself. It helps develop your personality. It will finally reflect on your business life as well.

A horse rider I know makes sense of the world when

comparing it to horse riding. It works almost perfectly. Musicians I know let go of their inner pressures with music. Running long distances do the same for others. All these things will help us to reflect who we are. You define yourself by the things you do.

These things change our view on life.

A job brings food to the table. It even may be rewarding. But you cannot develop it if you don't develop your personality.

Usually people describe me as a programmer who plays the Shakuhachi. But I am actually a Shakuhachi player who programs computers. In my life, I appreciate flowers and singing birds. I try to take a look out of the window even when the pressure is high. This is not only protecting myself or laziness. It helps me to be introspective. It helps me to find errors in my thinking. It helps me make my job better and set priorities. I am a Shakuhachi player even when I am not playing. I am one when I enter the meeting room. With every breath I am a Shakuhachi player. Even when my arms no longer work and I can't play anymore, I will stay one.

Who are you?

If you can't answer that, it's time to sit down, and reflect on your life.

Beginner's Mind

I once met some strange people. They were coming from a university and on their first day in the office they expected to become team leaders. Of course they didn't get what they wanted and were utterly disappointed.

They may have had the best grades at college, but on the job they most often needed to start from scratch. In university you probably learn about the Java programming language. On the job you need to learn about tons of new tools and new programming concepts.

Some young developers adapt to their situations quickly; some do not. They act with an expert's mind and it is incredibly difficult to educate an expert. Experts tend to believe they know everything already and can hardly accept any new knowledge. They learn slowly.

At some points I have accepted new team members who turned out to be of the "expert"-kind. Experienced or not, experts can be a poison to a project.

> In the beginner's mind there are many possibilities. In the expert's mind there are few.
>
> —Shunryu Suzuki (Suzuki, 2011)

Shunryu Suzuki speaks out of my heart. The more of an expert you are, the less options you can see. I was told when I was a young developer that "If you have a hammer, all problems look like a nail."

The colleague who told me that had a lot of experience, but didn't maintain an expert mind.

He always looked for the best tool or concept whenever

he faced a problem. He learned Perl for when he needed one-liners. He learned XSLT when he did XML transformations. He constantly learned new things and was not afraid to try something new. Constant learning does not only keep your mind fresh, it extends your horizons. It shows different solutions to the same problem and eventually you can choose the best from them.

There is a known issue with us "experts" which affects mostly customers.

When a new customer is showing us his requirements and we consider ourselves a domain expert, there is a chance we stop listening carefully. Without learning about the customers' thoughts we tend to give the same advice as we did before. Two car manufacturers might share a problem, but with their different backgrounds they might need different solutions.

Instead it is better to maintain a beginner's mind. Assume you have never worked for a customer like the one you are currently listening too. Assume you are a beginner at your favorite programming language. Assume there might something true in what the other guy tells you and listen. You don't need to adopt this knowledge, but you should listen as if a beginner.

Coding Like a Tenzo

A Tenzo is the cook of a Zen monastery. While in Europe the common "cook" is not associated with any special glory, the Tenzo is a highly respected person and has an important role in Zen.

Dōgen wrote quite a long text on the Tenzo. Master Dōgen was born in the year 1200. After the death of his mother, he joined a monastery. This time in Japan was characterized by (civil) war. Even the Zen monks were sometimes armed and acted as soldiers when the different Zen lineages wanted to achieve more power. Dōgen left the monastery early as he could not see the reflection of the Buddha-way in the life inside the monastery. After the civil war, he went to China to learn about the Buddha nature. Today he is known as the renovator of the Zen way and the patriarch of today's Sōtō lineage.

One of his works is the Tenzo-kyōkun, "Briefings for the Cook" (Dōgen, 2007). He wrote it because he thought cooking in many monstasteries was not done with the right awareness. He believed a Tenzo was important and his duties should be considered an important practice. Only the best students should have the honor of being a Tenzo.

When I read this text[34] years ago I realized that programmers should code like a Tenzo.

The Tenzo needs to calculate carefully the rice and other foods for the monks. There should be enough for everybody. There should be only a little left on the pan after each meal, but not too much. A Tenzo needs to look at the monks when he calculates the meal. How many are there? Are there guests? Are monks sick and unable to eat a lot? Are they doing hard work and need more? And so on.

---

[34] I actually read a German translation including comments from Kosho Uchiyama Roshi, who was a student of Kôdô Sawaki.

Programmers should act the same. As programmers we need to look at the requirements and calculate for ourselves how much effort is necessary. For example, if you are just creating a standard blog page with a simple setup it is most likely not necessary to create a detailed specification document or even a formal test plan. But it most likely is beneficial to make a few drawings for your customer to visualize what you are going to do. With that you have not done to little nor too much. If the project grows, you are still able to increase the number of specifications.

If you start with a bigger project, you should take care that things are tightly documented and there are enough specifications for the other team members. Documentation and specification is communication. You should write so much and so clearly that everybody can understand you. You are doing too much if you duplicate documentation. For example, copying parts of the documentation from the source code to a word processing file is often too much. There are tools available which let you generate documentation from one source and let you avoid the unnecessary effort.

A Tenzo has an overview of the kitchen. He knows what is missing and what is not. He takes time to think about these things and put them in order.

Like the Tenzo, Programmers need to keep an overview of the budget. They need to take time to recalculate and adjust their estimations. When asked, they need to be ready to give a proper response on the state of their activity at almost any time. As programmers we often face situations we cannot foresee. For example, when we wait for input from a customer. In these cases we need to be honest and open. In worst case, Tenzo programmers should not agree to projects when they know its participants will not be satisfied. The Tenzo might not cook when he doesn't have the ingredients.

The agile approach of computer programming tempts us to think only in blocks of programming time. If not applied with care, it doesn't respect creative time and the time you need to keep an eye on things. If there isn't enough time, the programmer should interfere. It's to be treated like any other risk on the budget we might have.

I once made a mistake when I agreed to a project which was low-budget and for which I didn't have the time. The customer constantly nagged on me until I agreed to hire a few students who would code his vision of a great new social network just for musicians. I knew the idea was not going to succeed. He told me he would be patient with the students, but I knew this wasn't going to be the case. The students wanted the job, and despite all of my bad feelings I finally told him we would do it. The only thing I did well was to keep control. But it didn't help me, I could see how quickly it went wrong. He became angry, and the students became angry. Finally I had to pay the students out of my own wallet.

Low budget projects never leave you the time to think twice or make good decisions. They don't give you the time for customer support. It's like cooking a soup without water.

Dōgen wrote, the Tenzo needs to prepare the food for the Sangha (the group of Zen monks) and should combine the six different tastes and the three preferences in harmony. The tastes are bitter, sour, sweet, salty, mild, and hot. The three preferences are right cooking, right preparation of the meal, and right taste. This is true for the Tenzo, but also for the programmer.

Programmers need to maintain balance between:

- complexity versus flexibility
- manual versus automated work
- documentation versus time-eating documents
- unit tests versus budget
- chaos versus methodology
- configuration versus convention

and so on.

We have to do it right. When a Tenzo finds a grain of sand in the rice, he must throw it away. He must not lose a single piece of rice when he cleans it. We must look at all our pros and cons and decide; we should take the best out of it, but don't let slip through hidden gems.

The Tenzo must cook carefully—he doesn't walk off and smoke a cigarette while the rice is boiling. He must serve the rice and the soup at the same time. He has helpers, but he is still responsible for everything becoming a success. To succeed he needs all of his attention and awareness. When we program or plan, we need awareness and concentration too. The preparation and planning of our project is as important as the execution.

We need to deliver the right taste; while the theory of test-driven development makes perfect sense, this is not true for each and every programming project. Don't get me wrong; unit tests are crucial for professional software development. But it might be better if you can deliver in time and budget with only the most complex parts unit tested than delivering four weeks late only because you wanted to test exceptions which cannot actually occur. Be honest about the risks of your source code. It might taste salty sometimes. It's not necessarily too salty. Unit testing should not become a religion, it is a tool.

Finally I would like to share a story from Dōgen's text which impressed me very much. I will leave interpretation up to you.

Dōgen said, the Tenzo does work with his full body and mind; he does not waste time and his work is a practice of the Buddha's teaching.

One day on his travels Dōgen arrived at a monastery. The sun was burning down without mercy and it was so hot that his feet could barely stand on the tiles. The Tenzo, Yung, was drying mushrooms. He carried a heavy bamboo stick and had no hat. He was sixty-eight years old and it was hard work for him. Dōgen could clearly see the sweat running into his eyes.

Dōgen asked: "Why do you not ask younger people to help you?" Yung answered: "Other people are not me." Dōgen did not think too long about this and asked again: "I think you are right, you are doing Buddha's work. But the heat is unbearable, why are you working when it is so hot?"

Yung responded: "Because now is the only time to act."

Karma Code

Karma is an important concept in many religions like Hinduism, Jainism, and Buddhism. It says that every action has a consequence, even actions of the mind. The butterfly effect claims a butterfly might cause a tropical storm with its wings. Karma is like that, just that it doesn't necessary have an effect on the current life but can affect one of the following.

Karma can be seen like math or physics principles. There is no god involved who judges you and your households by your Karma points.

In the Western world there is sometimes the misunderstanding that you should collect good Karma while avoiding bad Karma. This is not true. In fact, the ultimate goal is to not cause any Karma, good or bad. Like standing in the lake and not causing any disturbance; just being one with the lake and the environment.

Maybe you already have guessed, Buddhas do not cause Karma. If you do not create Karma anymore, you interrupt the countless cycles of birth and death and in the end you'll be released.

We need to write software without causing any Karma in the team or in the code. Good Karma and bad Karma both will cause waves and shake the persons involved.

Please forget what the terms "good" and "bad" mean in the Western world for now. You might think that "good" karma can only be beneficial, but it is not like that. "Good" karma are your good intentions which can do harm. Instead of trying to be "good" or even "bad", try to do the right thing. "Good" and "bad" are relative terms. What is good for you, is not always good to the one on the other table. Ethics is a complicated thing which does not have a clear answer. Acting "good" and "bad" leads to conflicts. "Acting without acting" is what we need to achieve.

Team Karma

Don't act arrogant or egotistical. The team is like a huge lake. You are a drop in the lake. If you behave badly, you become an oil drop and you become so toxic that you can poison a thousand gallons of water. You can cause the death of all the fish and birds living in the lake. If the lake is small enough, all life in the lake can die.

In the startup scene there are tons of blog posts about employee "number one". Startups are fragile ecosystems. They start small and sometimes have the luck to stay small. But sometimes they grow to huge dimensions. And it all starts with hire number one. The first hire is often seen as the most important hire as he dictates the tune and atmosphere in the team. You can cause bad karma if you decide to employ a brilliant ... jerk. Nobody wants to work with a jerk, even if he is a genius. Big companies might be able to compensate for that karma, but small companies might have a problem.

You could create good karma if you employ a nice, friendly person who loves his job and always has a positive attitude. If you are born with a smile on your face, you might not have a problem. But if you are sometimes introverted and cannot always see the positive side of something, the guy with the good karma can start getting on your nerves.

Being a jerk or being a sunshine is relative to the people who surround you.

It is optimal to hire a person that fits you and your team. The person is not exaggeratedly nice or negative compared to you and your team. He shares visions and dreams, but fills slots which are currently unmanned. Finding the right person is today's Art of Recruiting. In today's world of IT micro-businesses it is not only "fill up a free position".

Code Karma

If you write code which is flawed, you create bad karma. Bad karma will come back in this version or in a later version.

The wrong code can cause serious trouble in a startup and make it fail. You should avoid code which "fires back". If you would like to avoid bad code, I recommend the following books:

- "Clean Code" by Robert C. Martin (Martin, 2008)
- "Design Patterns" by Erich Gamma et al. (Gamma, 1995)
- "Refactoring" by Martin Fowler (Fowler, 2008)

You should have read these books in university already.

Bad karma in code might come through lack of unit testing, unreadable code, or an exaggerated complexity. Hungarian notation is no longer necessary in the times of modern IDEs. And complexity is a subjective matter which can be avoided by just discussing it with colleagues. Code reviews are really helpful to defeat brain farts.

You can avoid bad karma in code if you think twice on every line you type. Don't accept bad notations just because you don't know any other. If you learn about something, try to look up alternatives. Compare them. Develop your own opinion and change it, when somebody has better argumentation than you.

Bad karma in code can be found often by using appropriate tools. For example, Findbugs[35] can help you to spot quite a few bad smells in your code, like unwanted modification of objects. There are also unit test tools, code format checkers, and tools which tell you when something you wrote is simply too complex.

In other terms, bad karma code is created by bad code without much attention.

Code is not here to show what a great programmer you are. Code is just here to serve the purpose, fulfill the requirements, and to be maintainable. If you write code because you want to be praised for your skills you create good karma. You might have good intentions: making the most flexible system ever or create the most reusable testing system. But if there is no need for the these things, you are just complicating things.

---

[35]http://findbugs.sourceforge.net

In other terms, good karma code is created by good code with good intentions and the search for a reward. Code which is too good will turn out bad: if nobody in your team can understand it anymore it might be a fantastic system but useless.

Good karma in code is more problematic. The person who creates good karma does usually have good reasons for his decisions. A discussion is very hard and a consensus often even harder to find. For example, a brilliant but really geeky colleague once introduced graph theory for a business module. The whole proposal was utterly complex and hard to follow. You needed some good math skills and lots of time to get it. We didn't know if we would ever need the features this proposal would give to us as the requirements were unclear. But after some discussion, we agreed to use it.

We made two mistakes.

First, we had an expert's mindset. We should have looked at the problem with a beginner's mind. There was only one solution we discussed, but there might have been others.

Second, we created good karma because we thought way too far in the future. We added features we probably would need in five years. It is an often-used argument to spend more time now and save it later; this is also a really dangerous argument. You cannot argue against it.

In our case, karma fired back. The requirements changed slightly, and it caused our code to change too. We had a lot of exceptions suddenly and it was hard to maintain the code. Still, I have no idea how we could have made this better. I just know that, by taking some more time, we could have found a better way.

Good karma is caused by team members who want to create "something very, very good for the greater good." They craft the best, most flexible code they can. It's much more than one needs, but for them it's just the best thing one can have. Maybe there's some ego included as well, but not necessarily.

On another occasion I asked a developer to help somebody from the QA team with testing tools to lower their workload. The dev was highly motivated and started with the tools. The code became very flexible. So flexible that QA never used it. They would need to configure an Excel sheet with around 10,000 options to make a few tests. Yes, it was flexible and in theory it would have been what we needed. But it was far too much. It was all done with the best faith and knowledge the developer had.

Bad karma is much easier to avoid than good karma. While all karma is a result of us humans failing in one way or another, bad karma can be spotted and controlled with the use of tools. Good karma is not under the control of such tools. It is in many cases a social problem and one of passion. "Doing the best I can" is not always the best way to go. We all must sit down for a while and really try hard to match the actual requirements with what we can do considering the environment we are operating in. That said, preventing good karma can be achieved by looking at the project as a whole, including project members, customers, requirements, competitors, and our own selves.

To sum it up:

Bad Karma in code is created by bad code without caring. Good Karma in code is created by good code with your praise in mind.

It is better to create no karma.

You can create bad code even if you know what you are doing. Sometimes it is necessary to write flawed code. Everybody has done it and will do it. As long as you care about it, it is acceptable. People who care will fix the problem or have it in mind. They are able to react.

You can try to write extraordinarily good code. Focus on the problem you want to solve, not on what your coworkers might call you. A program should only solve the problem. If it is doing that but looks boring and generic it is most likely right.

The Other People

The Buddha Programmer

When I wrote "The Ten Rules of the Zen Programmer", somebody asked me: "How can one live and conform to all these rules?" Today I would prefer a different title more like: "Ten recommendations for Zen programming".

The term "rule" is demanding; it implies you are not a Zen Programmer if you break the rules. But it's not meant like that.

There are times when it is easy to commit to Zen. There are times it is very hard and we fail. Sometimes it is not possible to follow our own ethics or we need to work even when tired, just because we are afraid of the future. We are humans. In addition, if you are reading this book it is unlikely that you are a Zen monk—you probably have a job or are looking for one. Maybe you have to feed a family. It is very difficult to fulfill obligations while following the Zen way.

Monks step out of the life we all know. There still are many who practice Zen for a long time yet still do not master the way. How can we programmers, caught in stressful environments, expect to fully apply the Zen way?

A single book will not help. Quitting our job will not help and meditation for a couple of hours does not help. It is hard work and takes lifelong dedication to reach a balanced state of mind (exceptions of course may happen).

If you conform to all the rules, you have probably become a Buddha. One of those rare people with a clear sight. One of those people who always smiles. Compared to the teachings of such a person, this book is not of any value. I am far from being a Buddha programmer.

I wrote this book because Zen changed something in me. But this doesn't mean I am following my own rules all the time—I cannot. But I have become aware of my issues and have learned Zen is a way which might help me to figure them out.

I follow this way at my own pace. It is not the goal which makes us travel. The way alone should keep us moving. Becoming Buddha is not a goal and is not necessary. My goal is to keep my feet on the earth, as much as possible. I want to get out of the wheel of consumption, pressure, and deadlines. I want to live as a human being.

Buddhas are humans who stopped suffering. They are one with their environment. When looking at the real Buddhas of this world, something like a Buddha programmer does not exist. A Buddha wouldn't sit down to code things.

When I refer to Buddha programmers, it's just a term for a rare set of people. I don't connect them with real Buddhas, but to a person with clear sight and a calm mood. They see good things in their colleagues and speak about the bad things. If we are driven by emotions and desires, they help us find our way back. In general, these are the people others trust and love. They are not looking for followers or worshippers.

> If you meet Buddha on a road, kill him.
> —Linji Yixuan (Suzuki, 2011)

Linji Yixuan was the Founder of the Rinzai Zen lineage. The quote is one of his most popular sayings and you can find it referenced in many books. He thought this quote was so important that he used it in the first pages when explaining Zazen. If you see Buddha outside of you, it is a wrong Buddha. You need to get rid of it. You are not in the here and now but somewhere else. Kill the Buddha and you'll be free again. In other terms: if you want to become Buddha, you'll never attain Buddhahood. It is like this with programming: if you want to become a great programmer, it will be nearly impossible to become one. Chances are you become a jerk or a nitpicker. Instead, doing the best you can and enjoying work are the bones of any good programmer. It's the present which counts.

Having a goal can prevent your achieving it.

Practice for the sake of practice. Code for the sake of coding. I never heard a Zen master calling themselves "Buddha". Instead, everything "is" Buddha (Red Pine, 1987) or "has" Buddha nature (Dōgen, 1997). While animals express Buddhaness all the time, we humans need to learn to express it. Seeing it like that, you might consider "Buddhaness" a state of mind, which might even come and go. I don't know about that. But I know it's not useful to try to become either a great programmer or a Buddha (programmer).

Teacher and Student

Years ago, I called developers, from whom I learned much and who had a deep understanding of a specific technical area, "Guru". Later I moved to the term Sensei (Jap.: 先生). It means "born earlier". It expresses that I am also willing to learn how to approach a problem, not only the technical details.

A Sensei is the one who teaches you martial arts, Zen meditation, or whatever you want to learn. In Japan a Sensei has more weight than a teacher in the Western world.

A Sensei in Japan is more likened to an idol. Your relationship to a Sensei is much deeper, almost like the relation between parent and child. Once you have chosen your teacher, you will stick with him for a long while, probably forever. Leaving your Sensei is a serious thing though. If you leave your Sensei something terrible has happened. It is a sign of misrespect and lost trust. It is possible you will have trouble finding a new Sensei once you have left one.

In Zen people are often mentioned along with their teachers. For example: "Ushiyama Roshi, who was a student of Kôdô Sawaki ... "

On the other hand, a Sensei might release you if he feels

he can't do anything more for you. Years ago I read the phrase: "There will be a time you learn from a different Sensei." I forgot the name of the book and who said that. If you ever hear this from your Sensei you can consider it a huge compliment, because your Sensei just told you that you will become more skilled than he is.

But it seems the term can be used sarcastically in Japan. To avoid words which I cannot fully understand I use the term "teacher" for now.

Teachers in the West are different than the ones in Japan.

In the West, we do not necessarily have a relationship with a teacher. We go to a classroom and the teacher tries do his job by explaining some facts to us. When the show is over, we leave.

I, the Student

I never had such a strong relationship with the colleagues from whom I learned. But I tried to learn as much as possible. One day I was asked to join the EAI team. EAI means Enterprise Application Integration and it is the art of connecting huge software systems. It can be complicated and I was totally new to this field. Lucky for me, I had a competent teacher. He used a huge variety of tools and programming languages. He was not afraid to try something new or use a tool which he was not an expert with; he just tried to solve the problem in the most efficient way. In this way he learned a lot of new technologies. He was also very picky with his food and even selected the water he drank carefully. Even when we worked sixty, seventy hours and late into the night, he had a positive attitude and kept calm. We became a real team. I really tried to do things like he did. Later I would modify the way he worked so it would match my personal preference. For me it was fantastic and he had a huge impact on how I work today.

As his student, I tried to learn everything he was willing to teach. I listened and I imitated the way he worked.

Imitation often has a negative connotation in the Western world. It appears uncreative or less innovating. We forget this is the natural way of learning: our kids learn like that. When I started with playing Shakuhachi, I was asked to imitate until I got it. When I understood how the teacher played, I was allowed to experiment, recreate, and modify. To date, I have been imitating for four years. There is still much I don't get and need to take a closer look at.

There is a saying that when you start learning it's like letting bones grow. Later you build up muscles and nerves with imitation. When you get to skin, you have mastered your skill and can stop imitating.

I know a fantastic jazz piano player. We often discuss the nature of music. I told him a story of a rock band I know. The members of this band believe they could play music just with emotions. They say music theory is nothing they need to know about and refuse to even learn the basics. My jazz friend said, one needs to become an expert in music theory to be able to ignore the rules. This highlights the importance of imitating Bach or Vivaldi when you want to create experimental music. Without knowing the rules, you don't know how to break them.

While imitating, you already develop your own style. It is almost impossible not to do it. Imitating is not about cloning. I play the Shakuhachi very differently than my teacher, even when I try to sound like him.

As an aspiring student you can learn a lot of others. Many people are willing to teach you everything they know. I have learned that treating others with respect open a lot of doors. Making sure to think about questions and doing some research on your own before asking shows some more respect. Your teacher is not your personal Google search. Instead, providing one or more solutions and asking for confirmation is showing your motivation and interest. Teachers often reflect your behaviour. If you are lazy, teachers are lazy with answering questions. If you are interested in the matter and try your best, good teachers will help you to achieve the best.

Don't waste your teacher's time. Ask, what you need to ask, but do not feign interest by asking obvious questions. If you ask, prepare your questions for your teacher so it is easy to understand what you want to know. Keep the context short and precise and don't bore them with trivialities.

As mentioned, imitating is not cloning. My teacher used Perl one-liners and VI. I went home and tried it for a long time. While I never grew into Perl, I use VI a lot. Instead of Perl, I use Ruby.

A teacher often considers himself a student too. He might want to hear about your experiences. Coffee breaks are a good opportunity to speak about them. He might have a few more tips for you. He also most likely just loves to hear about your interests.

Never aim to get your teacher's job. Nobody will teach you anything again if you do. If you have success, make it also a success for your teacher. Do not forget, without him you wouldn't have come so far. It's not a shame to tell your team about the support of your teacher. In the moment you plan to get your teachers job or position, he is no longer your teacher. It will throw off the balance in your relationship.

Keep your relationship honest and open. If you have a problem with something your teacher does, tell him first. Do not upset him, just speak your mind and give him a chance to react. It's often a good idea to clarify positions with two sets of eyes, before discussing with a bigger audience.

If speaking is open and constructive, your teacher might rely on you. If you are not trying to make his failures your success, he will trust you. If that happens, you have completed a cycle and become the teacher of your teacher too.

Between Student and Teacher there is giving and taking. As a Student you do not have much knowledge to give. Therefore you must give trust, reliability, honesty, commitment, and loyalty.

On Teaching

One day I quit my job at a big consulting company and went to a smaller company. The teams only had a size of around 10 to fifteen people. The employees came from the local area and not from all over Germany. In many cases they were graduates. Without a doubt there were a lot of talented, young people in my team. Only the level of experience was concerning.

The first few days I was confused about a lot of problems that were discussed with me at my desk. I didn't have anybody to ask when I had questions and this made me feel alone. I felt a bit sad, because it felt as though I started teaching, but stopped learning at the same time.

Luckily, I was wrong.

I actually had a whole team to learn from. I found out it is true when somebody says "a teacher learns from his students."

For example, I learned what young employees consider difficult or easy to understand. It helped me to assign tasks. I also learned about the specific strengths of my colleagues. By looking at the individuals as a whole, I could assign specific roles so they made sense.

As a teacher I found out one should give advice like one puts salt in food: sparingly. Developers learn best from their own experience. Most often they are at the peak of mental development and body constitution. They have energy and a freshness which the older of us could use. There is no need for micro-management. They have the capability to solve problems on their own.

Teachers are already giving good advice when they simply act. If you want to explain the necessity of overtime, be the first one to work overtime. Good students will recognize what you do. Answer questions only when they ask. Even when you can see the question marks in their eyes, wait until they ask. Young colleagues need time to think. They will come to you when they need help.

It is said a Sensei teaches by letting the student make his or her own experiences. Eugen Herrigel was a Kyudo (Archery) student of Kenzo Awa and wrote:

"One day I asked the master: 'How can the shot be loosed if I do not do it?' 'It shoots,' he replied. 'I have heard you say that several times before, so let me put it another way: How can I wait self-obliviously for the shot if I am no longer there?' 'It waits at the highest tension.' 'And who or what is this It?' 'Once you have understood that, you will have no further need of me. And if I tried to give you a clue at the cost of your own experience, I should be the worst of teachers and should deserve to be sacked! So let's stop talking about it and go on practicing.' "

(see Herrigel, 1999))

The sole developer of a small project in my company needed somebody to review his code. I took the time and soon looked into tons of database commands and related programs. The way he developed was like running through the desert barefoot. Since he asked me to review his code, I told him there were software products which provide a more comfortable way to work with databases and recommended three of them. Some time later he thought it was a good idea to use such a tool and ported his code. He asked and decided himself. Today he has collected some great expert knowledge on a product which is highly demanded in today programming world. I ask him for advice from time to time. The decision to use such a database product and the fascination for the idea behind that kind of tool grew in him because he was interested and he had the chance to look into these things on his own. Balance between saying too little and too much is crucial.

The usual software trainers are just that: trainers. They don't feel responsibility for their students nor any kind of relation. It's all about slides and time paid. There are a few trainers who think differently. Students can feel they are taken seriously. It's about passion. The trainer is willing to change the regimen so it makes sense for the student. The best training sessions I joined were usually the ones where I kept in touch with the trainers. Sessions with "trainers" are wasted time; sessions with "teachers" are invaluable.

A teacher is responsible for the learning path. In my first days as an EAI developer, I did a lot of trivial tasks. When I had questions, I had them explained. My teacher was concerned and seriously interested in telling me everything I needed to know, even when these kind of questions must have bored him. He didn't overwhelm me with lectures, but waited until I had mastered what I had learned. Even when we were under pressure, he patiently waited for me until I could connect my knowledge and become a real help for him. After two years he left the project and a very thankful young programmer took over his role.

As a teacher, don't forget that your ego has no place in the relationship between you and your student. Kindness and patience is the key for successful learning.

If you feel that your student is not engaging much or enough, you should quit the teacher/student relationship and simply become his colleague. A relationship of this kind is two sided. Students who are driven by their own ego will never learn and cannot be helped. Avoid wasting your energy and time on people who are not willing to learn, and instead spend them on some more interesting things in your life.

A perfect teacher/student relationship is when the student becomes a teacher to the teacher himself.

Hungry Ghosts

When your company's motto is "up or out" people start to fight tooth and nail to earn a much as merit as possible. If you stop earning merit, your career has stopped too.

Projects in such an environment are often full of pointing fingers. If something went wrong, the person responsible wants to avoid any association with the problem. If somebody recognizes the problem, he will make sure he earns recognition for it. The one responsible will try to blame it on somebody else.

While this works in a way, the focus of a project is not the project itself, but the individual's career. Instead of teammates, such an environment creates competitors; competitors cannot congratulate others for success. Good ideas will look bad, even when there are no flaws.

When a company does not have such a motto, a single person who thinks like that might poison a project.

Projects like that easily lead to frustration and demotivation. There is an understanding that "competition" would be good in all cases. In fact, there is a difference between a good and healthy competition and one like I described. Creating a toxic atmosphere costs money. Too much pressure and frustration lead to errors. It makes people quit their jobs. And it's not easy to find good employees.

For me, the mythological "hungry ghost" from the earlier chapters perfectly describes people who are only focused on their own career. Hungry, because they feed on their career, which is just a fictitious word in a fictitious environment, and do not provide anything to hold their own weight. Ghost, because they seem to have forgotten how to live a human life and live only one aspect of their lives. From time to time, I have to defeat the hungry ghost in me too.

Once I was asked to supervise a second project. My company was short on people and the team was created by looking at who was available, not by skills. In a similar way the team leader was appointed. My boss simply asked who wanted to do the job. The one who responded first got it. The trouble began.

The customer was a big company and the new team leader was keen on keeping control of everything. He was never happy with the outcome of a single task. All communications to the customer must happen through him. Every task was checked by him. He became very angry when somebody did somthing which was not approved by him. It was a star setup of a team and he was the center of it.

When the team became bigger, the communication became harder. The customer's landscape was huge and complex. It was much simpler to manage and approve for a single person.

After a while, the team leader thought most others would not care enough about the project. He formed a sub-team with two trusted people to whom he complained often. The pressure grew and he became unhappy and stressed.

The team was unhappy too. While the customer recognized a hero developer, the team couldn't do a single thing right, had no positive feedback, and was not allowed to speak to other people, just like the customer.

After a while, the team leader left the company. I believe he thought he deserved a better team. He definitely thought the whole project would blow up when he left.

But it didn't. The atmosphere recovered and the project became a nicer place. A strong ego makes you believe that the world stops turning when you leave. But this is never the case. When the whole of mankind has gone, this world will keep on turning.

But how can one deal with a hungry ghost?

It is difficult. Hungry ghosts can become aggressive when they do not have enough food for their ego. I have actually never managed to bring a hungry ghost back to earth. They are just lost until they examine themselves, end in "total success" like becoming rich, or become a victim of burnout.

I have tried three ways.

Ignorance

I am not a kindergardener and I am not responsible for the behavior of other people. When I am a project manager, I am responsible for a good working atmosphere. But as long as I am not, it's hard to educate other people on their behavior. As a member in a big team I ignored a few hungry ghosts and tried to break this downward spiral by sticking to my own ethics. I simply said "thank you" when somebody helped me. I didn't make a secret of it. While the hungry ghosts climbed the ladder and others left the company, the pattern of ignorance helped me to stay in a good mood and on the project.

Ignoring hungry ghosts is not easy; they often hurt feelings. I tried to accept these feelings, but at the same time remembered that these emotions are just there because they are tied to my own ego.

Confrontation

This might work out when only a few people are hungry ghosts and if you have at least the same authority as them. When I tried it, I could not say I was perfectly happy with the outcome. It took a lot of energy out of me and made me unnecessarily tired. A private discussion didn't help so much; I had to confront the person before the team and, to be honest, it was a rough discussion. This prevented an escalation between the ghost and the rest of the team, but of course my relation to the ghost was worsened.

I can recommend confrontation only if there are no other options. In a heated discussion it is hard to keep balance, stay fair, and on topic.

Manipulation

Manipulation is a negative sounding term in most countries. I don't see it as being so negative. Every discussion is some kind of manipulation. If you want to make somebody understand your point of view, you are manipulating his thinking. You are manipulating even more when you want to convince somebody of something you believe in.

One can manipulate in a more negative vein. For example, excluding unliked people from a group. One can manipulate more positively when trying to calm a hectic situation.

There was a guy who always tried to excel me in meetings with our boss. No matter what I did, he always had a correction or criticism for me. He never told me before such meetings, only when our boss would see him. He saw me as his competitor and wanted to beat me. It was getting annoying and took away a lot of my productivity when I decided to just give him the credit he demanded. It was hard because I was upset. But I started to ask him more often for his opinions on a couple of solutions. He often chose the one I had in mind and, when we had a meeting, I highlighted how my colleague helped me to the satisfaction of our customer. It had two benefits: he would learn how I do things because I gave him more insight into my thoughts. It maybe helped him to be even more valuable to our company. And he soon learned so much that he could have a similar position as I had—on another project.

He became more relaxed as he was recognized. He also was nicer to me and even helped me in some situations. I somehow believe, he was happy that I helped him on his path, without ever saying. After all he got the role he wanted and we parted but kept a good relationship.

At the time of this writing, I am self employed. In many cases I can avoid working with hungry ghosts. I have refused jobs because I thought that the "ignore" pattern didn't help. Working in such toxic environments takes a lot of energy from me and makes my life worse. In addition, I consider it an incalculable risk factor in a project.

Incompetence

A project manager left the company and I had to take over his part. When we discussed the status of the project, he told me I needed to take care of Mike. Mike would make a lot of errors, worked slowly and didn't care about what he delivered. I was surprised. I knew Mike already and I always had the impression he was a nice and committed guy. Looking back, he had actually seemed a bit depressed.

On my first day alone, I took some time to speak to every team member. I asked them if they were happy with what they were doing. Mike said he was happy. I told him what the former project manager said. Then Mike told me, he was asked to work as a release manager, but he always wanted to work on the requirements. He liked to code, but he was afraid of the Unix shell. Being the release manager caused a huge discomfort for him, because he would be the last to check the release.

I didn't think Mike was incompetent. He just had the wrong job.

Later I learned there was somebody else who would love to be the release manager. This guy took over that role. Currently I was in charge of creating requirements. I asked Mike for help. He became an excellent communicator with the customer, wrote a ton of documents and at some point turned on his code editor to help the team with implementing a few features. He was a hybrid and knew a lot about our customers and also how our systems worked. His Unix skills didn't matter any longer.

He loved his new role. In no time the other team members respected him again and asked him for help when specifications were unclear.

It's hard to meet a truly incompetent person. I don't think I have ever met any. Instead I have met a lot people caught in the wrong job or role. It's easy to run a project with five developers and just release worse products. You need the "right people" for the job. You can try to switch roles, but maybe there is simply not the right person. Not everybody can do everything in the software landscape. This misunderstanding is causing a lot of trouble. A lot of recruiters think they can put a developer in any role they provide him. If it were like that, life would be much easier.

Computer programming is not only writing code. It's

speaking to the customer. It's translating technical terms to a human language. It's also calculating budget and estimation. It's planning complex software systems. Not everybody can be good at all of these skills. We try to highlight our competence on our business cards with less success. But what does it mean if somebody is a "Senior Chief Consultant" or a "Junior Web-Developer"? It basically means the "Senior Chief Consultant" is most likely not so good with dealing with HTML5 as the "Junior Web-Developer". It doesn't make the senior look incompetent if he fails at writing a nice looking HTML document.

Today, when I am staffing a project, I ask myself: is the candidate right for the project? Is this the role he wants?

Often we cannot roll dice and switch roles. We have to accept and need to go on. Times will change and situations will become better. We need to maintain a respectful tone and kindness, even when it is hard.

Only when the project is at risk, is there time to act. Speaking openly and honestly might help. If that doesn't help, we need to take the situation to the next level. Be aware that this will cause frustration and negative emotions—but probably not as much as a failing project.

Zenify Your Project

A project is like a huge row boat. It can carry a lot of people to a new destination. On its way the passengers will see many things like fantastic sunrises and thunderstorms, but also unknown creatures from the deep sea. People have a big influence. If everyone walks to the left side, the boat will tilt to left. If they all jump at the same time, the boat will bob. Sometimes everyone is at the helm and the boat is running through the water quickly. Sometimes nobody wants to take the rudder and everybody wants to be captain. Then the ship drifts aimlessly.

When the boat is damaged and the crew is frustrated, it can become a Titanic experience. While the project managers still claim the situation can be solved, developers might already be manning lifeboats.

The success of a project depends on the people. The crew—the manager, the tester, the requirements engineer, the programmer—they all have the duty to do their very best to keep the boat on course. Some other people are important even though they are not on the boat: customers. They are sending messages from the mainland to direct us where we need to go. We need to make our own way, following their advice as well as we can but passing dangerous places without damage.

Sun Tsu and the General

Sun Tsu was a Chinese philosopher and a general who lived around 500 BCE. He wrote a book with the title "The Art Of War" (Sun Tsu, 1988). This book does not teach you Zen as it is a military handbook. Sun Tsu died in 496 BCE, while Bodhidharma transmitted Zen (named Ch'an) to China around 480 CE. It is more likely that Sun Tsu was influenced by the strong influence of Confucius than by Buddhism.

Some lessons from Sun Tsu remind me of lessons I read from Master Takuan who instructed sword fighters in Zen. Sun Tsu's lessons do not touch Zen philosophy in any way, but they are valuable as they teach us to keep a clean and calm mind.

I want to refer to this book because it has a good story to tell:

> During the Warring States era, when the Wei general Wu Qi was military governor of West River, he wore the same clothes and ate the same food as the lowest of his soldiers. He did not use a mat to sit on, and he did not ride when traveling. He personally carried his own bundle of provisions and shared the toil and hardships of the soldiers. Once, when one of the soldiers was suffering from a festering wound on his arm, the general himself sucked out the pus. When that soldier's mother heard about this, she began to mourn. Someone said to her, "Your son is a soldier, yet the general himself sucked the pus from his wound - what is there to mourn about?"

The woman said, "Last year General Wu did the same thing for my husband, and as a result my husband fought in battle without taking a backward step, finally dying at the hands of an enemy. Now that the general has treated my son in this way too, I have no idea where he will die. This is why I mourn him."

—Sun Tsu

Good team leaders take care of their team, every single member. If you need to ask a lot of your team, you need to be the first to stand before them. You need to protect them from customers, the company, and whatever other problems might rise.

Good team leaders transform demanding overtime to something better. For example, a community evening event with some pizza and fun.

The Path of Ruin

Sun Tsu describes six mistakes generals can make which cause big trouble for their army. Leaders sometimes do not act mindfully but in anger. They might speak too much and do the wrong things.

When the general speaks unwisely to his officers, he sends anger down the hierarchy. People who become angry act rashly and do the wrong things. Bugfixes might be deployed without testing or cause an outage. Finally you bring anger home with you. Sun Tsu called this Ruin.

One day a manager told the team: "Shit always flows down." It was his way to tell us we had to do overtime and he wouldn't care. His boss might have told him to get new features done and now he is passing on the request. This a pretty perfect example for ruin.

Like in Sun Tsu's story of the wounded soldier, team leaders influence people. All people influence others, but these people do so even more. Anger might find its path through the hierarchy like in the following image.

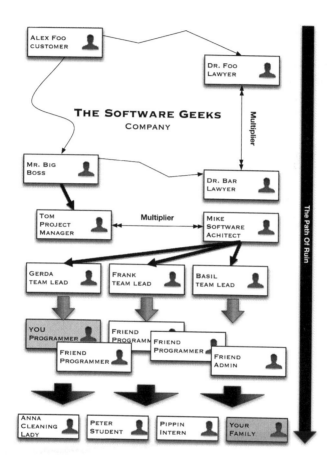

The Path of Ruin

"Family" is on the very bottom. It is on the same hierarchy as the cleaning lady or the intern. These share one thing: they mostly cannot defend against the problems from the upper levels.

Kids are often loud. After a long and hard working day it's very easy to have an emotional collapse and freak out even at the kids. If that happens, your work has caused something bad. You were not able to free your mind. Your family has to deal with it.

We need to take care to break the path of ruin. The flow must end when it reaches you. Don't shout at the intern just because you were not treated well. Don't shout at your family when they demand your attention just because you work on strategies to defeat your colleagues.

In Zen, we try to act mindful and with awareness. Only then can we stop the anger walking down the whole path. Stopping the wave of anger when it reaches us is the best we can do for our families and everybody else who interacts with us. Instead of passing it along we need to look at what happened and decide on the right action which sometimes is just accepting things as they are.

It's Never That Bad

When the boat is sinking and everything seems to be lost, remember one thing: you are alive. Most likely you can pay for food and your home. As a programmer, chances are good you are surviving a comlete failure of your project. Maybe you need to sell a few possessions, but most likely you'll need to get a new job. At least, it's like that in Germany. Interestingly I know a lot of people here who are afraid to lose their jobs.

While I wrote this book big parts of the world were struggling with an economic crisis. In Greece 27% of people need a job. In Germany it's just 5%. I get a lot of contracting offers. A lot of money is spent on infrastructure. Until now, I have not seen any real sign of an upcoming disaster for Germany. But a lot of people look at the bad situation in Greece and are afraid of losing their money. Sometimes they even speak as if Germany would stop existing tomorrow.

But why are we Germans complaining?

Greece is currently not a good place to be if you are young and want a future. Friends from Spain tell me worrying news too. A lot of talented and committed people can't find a job. It must be frustrating to live there. It is understandable why people there complain. It is not when Germans do. We are in a comfortable situation, but we also have a wrong outlook.

> If you don't have money, you have trouble. But it is good to know there are more important things than money. If you have no sexual desires something is wrong. But it is good to know there are more important things than sexual desires.
>
> —Kôdô Sawaki (Sawaki, 2007)

Kôshô Ushiyama explains what this quote means: if you believe you can solve any problem with money you become dependent on it (Sawaki, 2007). He wrote that he could end the Vietnam War given enough money. He simply would give all participating parties money until they stopped. Friends can be helped when they are in financial trouble. When old, he could become a nice old man with money. If he loses all of his money, nothing would be possible any more.

Kôdô Sawaki said in the same book, people make too much noise about earning their money. People say they are busy with getting their food on the table. But chickens are busy with their food too—just to be eaten again by humans. Money is an important tool in today's world. But it's nothing more than that. A tool. Nothing which we want to depend on.

It always impressed me that money doesn't really count in the world of a monk. I try to live as though money doesn't mean much to me too. I am honest; I fail. I am anxious when I don't earn enough in a month. I am dependent, even with a full bank account.

It is not easy to die from hunger where I live. If you are open to relocate you can almost certainly get some job. Maybe it will be underpaid, but you can have it.

If you don't find a job and are out of money you can beg.

Begging is for outcasts in the Western world. In Buddhism, having no belongings and begging is part of the religion. You can only live without dependence on money, if you give up everything you think you own. Monks practice every day to give up this dependency. Monks like

Kôdô Sawaki or Kôshô Ushiyama lived their whole life without owning anything. They never had holidays, they never traveled to Hawaii for a vacation. They didn't own TV and didn't think they needed a new laptop every two years.

Instead, they meditated, taught meditation, and begged.

When I was young, my father used to say: "If you don't learn anything in school you will become a beggar." In his mind, it would be the worst thing that could happen. But it is not. The worst thing that could happen is you starve and die from hunger. Or you have no safe place to sleep. There are a lot of people in this world who really suffer from a lack of safety and food. Even begging does not help. As long as you are not in such an situation, we can surely say that no matter happens, it is not as bad as it looks.

When the project gets bad, remember that. Things can go wrong. One does not need luxury to live a good life. Living a good life does not depend on a good job, a good role, or a high salary.

Things fail. If you have done the best you could do, there is no reason to be afraid.

Laugh When You Are Desperate

Laugh!

Laughing breaks the bars of almost every cage. In heated discussions, people focus more and more on their own beliefs, egos, and knowledge. Suddenly everybody is an expert. People easily get emotional, when their work is being criticized. In one hundred years our kids will laugh at us because our programming environment was so easy to understand and our business problems were trivial. We should laugh at ourselves more often, because we fight so hard for a lot of nonsense.

Don't take yourself so seriously. You are just some guy at some company doing some work. Reduce the pressure of your job: smiling does help. If the situation is terrible, look on the bright side and laugh. Let others participate.

I have been in several desperate situations where something was supposed to work—but it simply didn't! We searched for hours and almost gave up. Suddenly my colleague and I needed to laugh. I mean—two programming experts, a very simple use case which should just copy data from A to B. It was proven code, it must be related to a recent change which should be visible in the four lines which were touched. But we couldn't find it! After hours we just had to laugh, because it was ridiculous.

Honestly we laughed a bit hysterically. It was early in the morning. We had almost been on the job for twenty-four hours. I thought we would have all reasons to be desperate after all those hours. We made jokes about our stupidity and considered working as shepherds in Australia.

Laughing broke some mental barrier. Suddenly we spotted the error. Even programming beginners could fix it, it was so easy. But we were experts and that was most likely the problem.

One day I was interviewing an aspiring developer

asking him questions on various technical topics. He was very shy and it was clear that he was more concerned about the overall situation than what we really talked about. He tried to behave the same way as me. In addition he was sitting very straight and was worried about each and every word he was saying. When I noticed this, I was noticing myself. I had had a pretty bad start this day; I woke up way too late, I didn't manage to send an important letter, and I almost missed an important appointment. That is something which usually never happens to me. My stomach hurt a bit and generally I slept very poorly. So I must have looked like a serious, maybe grim guy, focused on work. My wife always tells me my deep voice can scare people. When I realized that, I decided to do an experiment. I sat back and made an open posture like I had seen in a book on body language. I quickly looked outside the window; the weather was great and warm. I had a good cup of coffee in front of me and actually was able to go to the post office during my lunch time: no need for hurry. Then I smiled. There once was a day I was in the same situation as this guy. I asked him if he did sports, because he looked athletic. This unexpected change of conversation confused him at first, but speaking of his favorite sports made him feel better. The whole atmosphere was more comfortable and we had a nice conversation. And I found out he was a talented guy and gave him the job he wanted.

Failing is an option. It happens often.

What matters is how we fail. We can despair or learn from our failures. Let's fail with a smile and do it better next time.

Some people say, "failure is not an option". But speaking like this doesn't prevent failing. It's not even motivating.

We cannot rule out failure and mistakes. There will always be bugs and wrong decisions. If we fail, we fail. If we succeed, we succeed. Do the best you can, then you can go on without worrying. Even when you fail, birds still sing and flowers are still beautiful. We don't live only inside a project; we are not only programmers, but humans. As such, the project is just a small event in our life.

Smiling is probably the greatest way to deal with problems.

The Ten Rules of a Zen Programmer

On a rainy morning I found myself sitting at my desk thinking about efficient working. Before I started as a freelancer, I had some days where I worked a lot but was never happy with the result. I started with Zen practice back in 2006. What came to my mind after a good while was: the old Zen masters already knew hundreds of years ago, how today's programmers should work. Even though I don't like these "be a better programmer" posts, I want to outline some of my thoughts from that time. It shall serve as a reminder for me, but if you have more ideas, feel free to comment.

1. Focus

If you have decided to work on a task, do it as well as you can. Don't start multiple things at the same time. Do only one thing at one time. You won't become faster or better, you'll just spread yourself too thin. If you work too much you'll become exhausted, make more errors and lose time jumping from one task to another. This is not only about programming; this is a general tip.

Kôdô Sawaki says: if you need to sleep, sleep. Don't plan your software when you are trying to sleep. Just sleep. If you code, code. Don't daydream—code. If you are so tired that you cannot program, sleep. Even known multitaskers like Stephan Uhrenbacher have decided to work singlethreaded. I had a similar experience to Stephan, when I finally wrote Time & Bill, a time tracking tool. My goal was to track my time so easily that I could do it even for small tasks like a phone call. Now I can create a few stopwatches at the beginning of the day and track my time with only one click. In the beginning it was a disaster: sometimes I just worked a few minutes on a task until I moved on to the next one. Now I am better. Similar to the Pomodoro technique I plan a few time slots and concentrate on them. No chatting, no sleeping, no checking out a great new game in the Appstore.

2. Keep Your Mind Clear

Before you work on your software, you need to clean up your mind. Throw away everything in your mind for the time being. If you have trouble with something, don't let it influence you. In most cases that trouble will go away. If the trouble is so much that you can't let it go, don't work. Try to clean things up. But when you start working, let the outer world melt away.

Something exciting on the mailing list? Leave it there. You can follow the exciting stuff later. Shutdown what fills your mind with shit: close Twitter, Facebook, your emails. You should even mute your phone and leave it in your pocket. You could say it is similar to item 1, focus. But there is one more restriction: don't use these tools before work or at lunch. They connect you with the outer world and bring up some new trouble or things which require you attention.

Think like this: at most times your mind is pretty clear when you wake up at the morning. If it is not, doing some sports helps (I do long-distance running). If you feel clean and refreshed, go to work and work as well as you can. When you leave your work then you can fill up your mind with clutter. You'll see it is not so much fun if you have a full working day behind you. Twitter and Co. are consuming much of your energy. Don't think it just takes a minute. It doesn't.

You know it's true.

3. Beginner's Mind

Remember the days when you were a beginner or if you are still a beginner, hold on to that feeling. You have never learned enough. If you are already an expert, think of yourself as though you were a beginner every day. Always try to see technologies from a beginner's mind. You can accept corrections to your software better and leave the standard path if you need to more easily. There are some good ideas even from people who don't have your experience. Was there ever a software built twice the same way? Even if you copy software it is somehow different.

4. No Ego

Some programmers have a huge problem: their own ego. But there is no time for developing an ego. There is no time for being a rockstar.

Who is it who decides your quality as programmer? You? No. Others? Probably. But can you really compare apples and bananas? No. You are an individual. You cannot compare your whole self with another human being. You can only compare a few facets.

A skill is nothing you can be proud of. You are good at Java? Cool. Someone else is not as good as you, but better at bowling. Is Java more important than bowling? It depends on the situation. You probably earn more money with Java, but the other guy might have more fun in life because of his bowling friends.

Can you really be proud that you are a geek? Programmers with ego don't learn. Learn from everybody, from the experienced and from the noobs at the same time.

Kôdô Sawaki once said: "You are not important."

Think about it.

5. There Is No Career Goal

If you want to gain something and don't care about your life "now", you have already lost the game. Just act as well as you can, without looking at the goal you might reach after a long time.

Working for twenty years to become the partner of a

company? Why aren't you working as hard as possible just because it is fun? Hard work can be fun. "A day without work is a day without food" is a Zen saying.

There is no need to start being happy after twenty years. You can be happy right now, even if you aren't a partner or don't drive a Porsche. Things change too easily. You can get sick. You can get fired. You can burn out (if you follow all these items I guess the likeliness is low).

Unless these bad things happen, just work as well as you can and have fun doing it. No reason to look at the gains of your colleagues. No reason to think about the cool new position which you didn't get.

After all, you will achieve something. You'll end up with nice memories, maybe a good position—and twenty excellent years. Every day is a good day.

If you ever come to the point where you think that working at your company is no fun at all you must leave immediately. NEVER stay at a company which takes away the happiness in your life. Of course, this is only possible in rich countries, where people have the choice to go away. But if you are living in such an good environment, do it. Go away without regret. You have no time to waste, you could be dead tomorrow.

When you have no career goal, going away is easy.

6. Shut Up

If you don't have anything to say, don't waste the time of your colleagues. This doesn't make you look wimpy. Every day you work you need to try not to get on someone else's nerves. Imagine if everybody would try this—what a great working place would that be? Sometimes it is not possible. Try hard, you will like it.

If you don't develop an ego it is pretty easy to shut up and care only for the things you can talk about. Don't mix up your ego with your "experience" and always remember: you are a beginner. If somebody has a good idea, support the idea.

7. Mindfulness. Care. Awareness.

Yes, you are working. But at the same time you are living and breathing. Even when you have some hard times at work you need to listen to the signs of your body. You need to learn about the things which are good for you. This includes everything, including basic things like food. You need to care for yourself and for everything in your environment—because after all, the water you drink is the water which runs in the river. You are living only for yourself. You live alone and you'll die alone. The world goes on even without you.

Avoid working in situations you don't like. Avoid working for free if it means you will have no fun and keeps you away from your bed. Let go what doesn't make you happy. Do you think people only work for free in theory? Consider the people doing Open Source in their free time. If you have subscribed to some project's mailing list you probably know what conflict there is (sometimes). If you don't have fun with it, stop doing it. I know a bunch of people who work in an Open Source environment they don't like. Again with Time & Bill I tracked the time I spent in Open Source projects and was surprised how much time I lost there—especially on projects I didn't like so much.

Keeping this in mind, some people think they are only happy when they have free time and can spend the evening with an Xbox and some beer. While this is a good idea from time to time, it is not necessary that every moment in your life is "fun". If you can avoid situations you don't like, avoid them. But sometimes there is need to do something really shitty. For example, manually copy/pasting stuff from your manager's Excel spreadsheet into phpmyadmin. This can take you days, and it is really boring. It is no fun, but sometimes you need to do such stuff. You cannot always quit your job when you get a boring task. Zen Monks do not shy from their work either. They get up at 3am (sometimes earlier, sometimes later, depends on the convent) and start meditation and work (they even consider work meditation practice). They have stuff to do like cleaning the toilets. Or working in the garden. Or as a Tenzo, they cook. They do it with all the care they can muster. Whatever they do, they do it without suffering and they are (or should be) happy, because every second, even the moments where they are cleaning toilets, is a second of their life.

That being said: stop whining if you need to copy/paste Excel. Just do it. Don't waste your energy with such things; they will pass. Become the best Excel copy/paster out there instead.

If you suffer a heart attack, people will probably say: "Uh yes, he really was a hard worker—he even worked for me for free at night". Nobody can guide you to the other world. This last step is taken by us alone. You cannot exchange anything in this world. Not even a fart. So it is up to you to take care, every second. If you die, you die. But when you live, you live. There is no time to waste.

"Care" is a huge word in Zen Buddhism (and I think in every form of Buddhism). I cannot express everything which needs to be said. it is difficult to understand the different meanings of "care". You are probably better off with the word "awareness". You must be aware of what you do, in every second of your life. You must be mindful in your life. Otherwise you waste it. But, of course, it is up to you to do so, if you like.

8. There Is No Boss

Yes, there is somebody who pays you. There is somebody who tells you what needs to be done. And he can fire you. But this is no reason to give up your own life or to become sick of your work. Finally, your boss has no control over you. It can even be doubted that you have control over you—but don't go down this path.

Back to your boss: he can make your life worse if you allow him to do so. But there is a way out. Say "No" if you need to do something which makes you sick or is against your ethics. What will happen? Worst case scenario he will fire you. So what? If you live in Western nations and if you are a coder (which is very likely if you are reading this) you'll get another job.

I don't mean say "No" to tasks like copying CSV Data to HTML. I am speaking of eighty-hour weeks and feeling your body break down. Or feeling that your kids need some attention too. Or if you are forced to fire people just because your boss doesn't like them. Or if you are a consultant and get the job to develop software for nuclear plants (some might say it is perfectly fine to work for nuclear power companies— it is against my ethics and serves as an example) or for tanks. You can say "No".

9. Do Something Else

A programmer is more than a programmer. You should do something which has nothing to do with computers. In your free time, go sailing, fishing, diving. Do meditation, martial arts. Play Shakuhachi. Whatever you do, do it with all the power you have left. Like you do in your work time. Do it seriously. A hobby is not just a hobby, it's an expression of who you are. Don't let anybody fool you, when they say hobbies are not important. Nowadays we can afford having hobbies. I have recorded several CDs and wrote fantasy books (the latter one unpublished, I must practice more). These things have made me the person I am now, and finally they have led me to Zen and this book. These days I practice Zen Shakuhachi. It is a very important aspect of my daily life.

10. There Is Nothing Special

A flower is beauty. But it's just a beautiful flower—nothing more. There is nothing special about it. You are a human who can program. Maybe you are good. There is nothing special about you. You are of the same stuff as I am and all the others on this planet.

You need to go to the toilet and you need to eat. Of course you need to sleep. After (hopefully) a long time you will die and everything you have created will be lost. Even pyramids get lost, after a long time. Do you know the names of the people who built them? If you do, is it important that you know? It's not. Pyramids are there, or they aren't. Nothing special.

Same goes for your software. The bank is earning money with your software. After you leave, nobody remembers you. There is nothing wrong about that. It is the flow of time. Nothing you should be worried about it. If you are following the first nine rules, you'll see that this last project was a good and fun project. Now it's simply time to go on and concentrate on something else.

If your company closes because of financial problems, no problem. Life will go on. There is no real need for an Xbox, a car, or something else. Most people on this planet live in deepest poverty. They don't care for an Xbox because they would be glad to get some food or even water.

So... why exactly are you special? Because you had the luck to be born in a Western country? Because you can code? No, there is nothing special about it. You can let go of your ego and live freely. Enjoy the colors and the smell of flowers. Don't be too sad when the winter arrives and don't be too happy when spring comes back. It is just a flow. Keep it in mind when somebody denies your application. Because no company is so special that you need to be worried about the job.

What Now?

You just read a book which explains Zen to Programmers. The question is, why you did that. People who are reading about Zen are usually searching for something.

Zen is a trending term within the developer community. It's often used as a synonym for "minimal," "efficient," or "productivity." But this book doesn't aim to make you work harder. This book is intended to give you some inspiration on how to live better. This may of course positively reflect in your work—it happened to me.

When I started with Zen, I hoped I could find some magic recipe which could help me withstand stress. The bad news: there is no magic recipe. Zen did not solve my problems. The good news: Zen showed me that I am the only person who is able to solve my problems.

The problems I had were problems of my mind. I had to clean it. In computer terms: I needed to reboot my operating system. I believed my problem was unique and couldn't be compared to anything else. The search for a solution might have lead to therapists, self-help books, gurus, or even just a couple of beers. But after I had practiced for a while, I distanced myself from my problem and understood that it was just me who could solve it. I could not change the company nor the project. It was me who needed to change. This book cannot make you act.

In the end no book, no guru, no friend can change your

life. You alone are responsible for this.

> There is no 'way to peace,' there is only 'peace.' "
>
> —-Mahatma Gandhi

Our feelings are our *reality*. If you feel something is wrong, then there is something wrong. In the noise of exhausting business days I could not hear the voice which warned me. I needed Zen to able to listen. Zen didn't decide for me. It made me listen.

It is easy to forget our mortality. When I was young, a friend asked me: "Could you accept your death right now?" I couldn't. I had dreams. I wanted to achieve something. If a truck had hit me, you would have seen surprise in my eyes. As a young man, I felt immortal. I worked hard and harder and forgot my real life. I lived inside a theoretical construct, a jail made up from my mind. I gave it too much weight and importance.

Even now I sometimes forget real life. When I consider the success of a company more important than my own breathing and health, then I need to meditate more often. Besides meditation, I use the techniques mentioned in this book. Not all at one time, just when it makes sense. With time you will develop your own techniques.

I know a women who is mastering her life through horses. When she feels lost, she drives to the nearby ranch and cares for her horses. I am not speaking of riding sports.

It is an intense relationship between horse and woman. It gives her the necessary distance. When you look closely at this relationship, you'll find similar elements as in Zen meditation. In Zen there is not only sitting meditation, there is a tea and a gardening meditation as well. Why shouldn't there be a horse meditation?

I am not saying you need a hobby. I am speaking of making sense of life. I am speaking of finding "your way."

Teachers like Kôdô Sawaki emphasized the value of sitting meditation their whole life. It's now perfectly clear to me: without silence and concentration, you will drown in an ocean of noise. I am following the way of the bamboo flute. What is your way?

Start small: take just ten minutes a day. Sit down in a chair of your choice where nobody disturbs you. Choose a nice place where you feel comfortable. Just sit there and do nothing. No emails. No phone. When thoughts come, let them pass. Don't start to believe this time is for making plans. You will fail miserably at first. But the more often you do it, the better you become.

I wake up at 5am every day. While the coffee is brewing, I take a moment to breathe the morning air and enjoy my existence. These are my ten minutes.

Ten minutes just for you will change you after a while. If you really want to change your life, you should start with these ten minutes. If you manage that, you'll find your way.

Good luck and thanks for reading.

Bibliography

Red Pine (Eds). (1987). The Zen Teaching of Bodhidharma. New York: North Point Press, 1989.

Kôdô Sawaki. (2005). An Dich. Frankfurt: Angkor Verlag.

Kôdô Sawaki. (2005). Zen ist die größte Lüge aller Zeiten. Frankfurt: Angkor Verlag.

Kôdô Sawaki. (2008). Tag für Tag ein guter Tag. Frankfurt: Angkor Verlag. ISBN: 978-3-936018-57-8

Kôdô Sawaki, Kosho Ushiyama. (2007). Die Zen-Lehre des Landstreichers Kôdô. Frankfurt: Angkor Verlag.

Dhammasaavaka. (2005). The Buddhism Primer: An Introduction to Buddhism. Boston: Lulu.com. ISBN: 1-4116-6334-9

Jiho Sargent. (2001). Asking About Zen: 108 Answers. Boston: Weatherhill. ISBN: 0-7567-8888-9

Siddharta Gautama Buddha. Editorial Committee, Burma Tipitaka Association Rangoon (Eds.). (1986). The Dhammapada: Verses and Stories. Retrieved April 2, 2013, from: http://goo.gl/wIDPKI

Immanuel Kant. Grundlegung zur Metaphysik der Sitten. (2004). Göttingen: Vandenhoeck and Ruprecht. ISBN: 3-525-30602-4

A. B. Mitford. (2005). Tales of Old Japan: Folklore, Fairy Tales, Ghost Stories and Legends of the Samurai. Dover

Pubn Inc. ISBN: 978-0486440620

Matthias Burisch. (2006). Das Burnout-Syndrom, 3. Auflage. Heidelberg: Springer Medizin Verlag. ISBN: 3-540-23718-6

Frank Gebert. (2010). Wenn Arbeit krank macht. FOCUS Magazin 10.2010. Retrieved April 6, 2013, from goo.gl/WfgAM9

M. Kläsgen. (2010). Selbstmord in Serie. Retrieved April 6, 2013, from: http://goo.gl/ePYrb3

BBC News Europe. (2012). Ex-France Telecom chief Lombard probed over suicided. Retreived August 23, 2012, from: http://goo.gl/DoMKAO

DAK-Gesundheitsreport Hamburg. (2010). Retrieved April 6, 2013, from: http://goo.gl/WDn0yl

Andrea Lohmann-Haislah: Stressreport Deutschland 2012. Psychische Anforderungen, Ressourcen und Befinden. 1. Auflage. Dortmund: Bundesanstalt für Arbeitsschutz und Arbeitsmedizin 2012; ISBN: 978-3-88261-725-2

Shunryu Suzuki: Zen Mind, Beginners's Mind. 2011. Shambhala; ISBN: 978-1-59030-849-3

LAM TE NGU LUC: The Sayings of Zen Master Linji Yixuan. Rctrieved 15.04.2013 from: http://goo.gl/x01t6P

Lafcadio Hearn: Kwaidan. Stories and Studies of Strange Things. Boston: Houghton, Mifflin and Co. 1904. Retrieved 23.07.2013 from: http://goo.gl/OtaE9a

Brad Isaac: Jerry Seinfeld's Productivity Secret. Lifehacker. Retrieved July 02, 2013, from: http://goo.gl/CK9sNE

Gerald M. Weinberg: The Psychology of Computer Programming. Van Nostrand Reinhold Company. 1972. ISBN:

978-0-44229-264-5

Eugen Herrigel: Zen and the Art of Archery. 1999. Vintage Books. ISBN: 0-3757-0509-0

Dōgen: Shobogenzo Zuimonki. Kristkeitz; Auflage: 4., durchgesehene und überarbeitete Auflage. 1997. ISBN: 3-9323-3768-9

Sun Tsu: The Art Of War: Complete Text and Commentaries. 1988. Boston: Shambhala Publications, Inc. ISBN: 978-1-59030-054-1

Forsyth, D. R.: Group Dynamics. 5th ed. 2009. Pacific Grove, CA: Brooks/Cole.

Watazumi Roshi: The Way of Watzumi. Retrieved November 25, 2012, from: http://goo.gl/c96gkl

Friedrich Nietzsche: Jenseits von Gut und Böse. 1886.

Dōgen, Kosho Uchiyama Roshi: Zen für Küche und Garten. 2007. Frankfurt: Angkor Verlag

Charles W. Eliot: The Sayings of Confucius. Vol. XLIV, Part 1. The Harvard Classics. New York: P.F. Collier & Son, 1909–14; Bartleby.com, 2001. www.bartleby.com/44/1/.

Patrick McKenzie: Don't Call Yourself A Programmer, And Other Career Advice. Retrieved October 28, 2011, from: http://goo.gl/SwGcjH

Johnson, R. and Gamma, E. and Vlissides, J. and Helm, R.: Design Patterns: Elements of Reusable Object-Oriented Software. 1995. Addison-Wesley. ISBN: 9-780-20163-361-0

Robert C. Martin: Clean Code: A Handbook of Agile Software Craftsmanship. 2008. Prentice Hall PTR. ISBN: 0-1323-5088-2

Martin Fowler: Refactoring: Improving the Design of

Existing Code. Don Wells and Laurie A. Williams (Eds.).
2002. London, UK: Springer-Verlag.

Made in the USA
Coppell, TX
13 December 2021

68392727R00129